DISABILITY DISCRIMINATION: LAW AND LITIGATION

by Andrew Hogan LLM
Barrister-at-Law

Published by
EMIS Professional Publishing Ltd
31–33 Stonehills House
Welwyn Garden City
Hertfordshire
AL8 6PU

ISBN 1 85811 237 0

Typeset by Tracey Dabell.

Cover design by Jane Conway.

Printed and bound in the UK by J W Arrowsmith.

For my wife

CONTENTS

TABLE OF CASES

TABLE OF STATUTES

TABLE OF STATUTORY INSTRUMENTS AND GUIDANCE

CHAPTER ONE
THE LEGISLATIVE FRAMEWORK

SYNOPSIS

This chapter examines the legal framework within which claims for disability discrimination will be brought. It considers briefly the three principal statutes comprising that framework including the Disability Rights Commission Act 1999, the Human Rights Act 1998 and the Disability Discrimination Act 1995. It also notes the various *Codes, Guidance* and secondary legislation made under the latter of these Acts, to which regard must be had.

THE CONCEPTS

The common law of England and Wales does not recognise any vehicle of redress for disabled people in respect of discrimination. Disability discrimination litigation within the jurisdiction takes place within a statutory framework and accordingly it is the statutes and secondary sources of law, which derive from them, which must be considered.

In practical terms the disability discrimination lawyer, or the lawyer confronted with resisting a discrimination claim, must have regard to the cornerstone of the statutory framework, the Disability Discrimination Act 1995 ("the DDA 1995"); the statutory instruments made under the DDA 1995; several *Codes of Practice* issued, to date, under provisions of the DDA 1995; and *Guidance* on the meaning of disability.

In addition, the government through the Disability Rights Commission Act 1999 ("the DRCA 1999") has established a Disability Rights Commission to further the cause of disabled people and this has also modified the framework established by the DDA 1995. Finally regard must be had to the

Human Rights Act 1998 ("the HRA 1998") which only came into force in October 2000, but which will have significant implications for the rights of disabled people in this country and also in enforcing those rights through litigation.

THE DISABILITY DISCRIMINATION ACT 1995

The DDA 1995 provides a framework to provide redress for disabled people who have been discriminated against in various spheres. **Part I** (with Schedule 1) establishes the criteria for determining who is disabled and afforded the protection of the Act.

Part II is concerned with discrimination in the employment field by employers or prospective employers, with provision made to extend the ambit of discrimination protection to include contract workers and trade organisations, specific provisions dealing with leasehold premises, occupational pension schemes and insurance services. The employment tribunal is the venue for litigation arising out of these provisions.

Part III is concerned with providing remedies for discrimination against disabled members of the general public in the provision of goods and services. Claims arising from discrimination in this field will be the subject of litigation in the county court.

Parts IV and V are concerned with the provision of education for disabled people and with public transport use. The DDA 1995 does not provide for direct action to be taken against education providers or public transport providers, but rather is concerned to promote greater provision for disabled persons.

Part VI deals with the establishment of the National Disability Council, now superseded by the Disability Rights Commission.

THE SECONDARY LEGISLATION

The DDA 1995 has generated a wealth of secondary legislation, which either brings into effect the provisions of the Act or clarifies or details the application of the provisions within the Act. Not all of the DDA 1995 is in force and accordingly regard must be had to the commencement dates of the various sections. The most important of the regulations are:

- Disability Discrimination (Meaning of Disability) Regulations 1996, SI 1996/1455
- Disability Discrimination (Questions and Replies) Order 1996, SI 1996/2793
- Disability Discrimination (Employment) Regulations 1996, SI 1996/1456
- Disability Discrimination (Exemption for Small Employers) Order 1998, SI 1998/2618
- Disability Discrimination (Services and Premises) Regulations 1996, SI 1996/1836
- Disability Discrimination (Sub-leases and Sub-tenancies) Regulations 1996, SI 1996/1333

These are the Regulations to which most regard will commonly have to be had, but practitioners should be aware there are other Regulations including the various Commencement Orders.

THE CODES OF PRACTICE

Under the provisions of the DDA 1995, particularly sections 51 and 53, the Secretary of State has power to issue *Codes of Practice*. *Codes of Practice* relating to employment matters were issued under section 53, and were intended to eliminate discrimination and encourage good practice. The emphasis of the *Code* as provided by section 53(3) is to provide practical guidance. The *Code* has statutory admissibility under section 53(5) and has to be taken into account by an employment tribunal or court, if its provisions are relevant.

In relation to other areas, such as the field of goods and services, the provision for issuing a *Code of Practice* differed slightly, in that pursuant to section 51 of the DDA 1995, the National Disability Council prepared the code which was then approved after consultation. These sections were repealed by the DRC 1999, which replaced them with a new section 53A, which allocated responsibility for the preparation of future codes to the Disability Rights Commission.

The *Codes* are of immense practical significance in the context of litigation as they establish what an employment tribunal will normally find to be acceptable employment practice in the context of a disabled person. Little if any use of the relevant *Codes* has been made in county court litigation. The principal *Codes* are:

- Code of Practice for the elimination of discrimination in the field of employment against disabled persons or persons who have had a disability. (ISBN: 0112710557).
- Code of Practice: Rights of Access, Goods, Facilities, Services and Premises. (ISBN: 0117624322).
- Code of Practice: Duties of trade organisations to their disabled members and applicants. (ISBN: 0112710719).

THE STATUTORY GUIDANCE

Part I of the DDA 1995 is concerned with defining who is disabled and accordingly entitled to the protection of the Act. The criteria for establishing who is disabled are drawn from three sources. The first of these is section 1 of the DDA 1995. The second is the Disability Discrimination (Meaning of Disability) Regulations 1996, SI 1996/1455. The third is a document entitled *Guidance on matters to be taken into account in determining questions relating to the definition of disability* (ISBN: 01127009559).

This document was issued by the Secretary of State pursuant to his power to do so under section 3 of the DDA 1995. The purpose of the document is to provide guidance to clarify the definition of disability contained in section 1. It is also intended to provide examples from which an employment tribunal or court can draw assistance in determining the issue of disability and it is mandatory, by reason of section 3(3), that an employment tribunal or court take it into account when adjudicating on issues to which it is relevant.

THE HUMAN RIGHTS ACT 1998

The HRA 1998 was brought into force in October 2000. It brings into the sphere of domestic law the European Convention on Human Rights. The key provisions of the Act provide first that all legislation must be interpreted and given effect to, as far as is possible, in accordance with Convention rights. Secondly it is unlawful for a public authority to act incompatibly with

Convention rights and a new statutory tort is created allowing a direct action to be brought on the right alleged to have been breached. Thirdly UK courts must take account of Convention Rights in all cases that come before them. The common law must be developed in accordance with the Convention, and decisions made by the European Court of Human Rights, whilst not binding, must be taken into account.

Much has been written about (as well as for and against) the HRA 1998, but whilst much debate has focussed on such issues as to whether or not the HRA 1998 has full "horizontal effect" between individuals or indirect effect through the mechanism of the courts, relatively little has been written as to the practical actions which can be launched to obtain money and other remedies, which could not be undertaken prior to October 2000. This book in its concluding chapters will consider the "New Model" of human rights litigation, together with suggested test cases.

THE DISABILITY RIGHTS COMMISSION ACT 1999

The National Disability Council established by the DDA 1995 was in no way comparable to the Equal Opportunities Commission or the Commission for Racial Equality. It was an advisory body. As a result, the DDA 1995 lacked a motive force for its enforcement and the further development of disability discrimination law. The Disability Rights Commission was created by the DRC 1999 to remedy this deficiency and to ensure that disability rights remained on the agenda. Section 2(1) of the DRC 1999 specifies the Commission's duties:

- to work towards the elimination of discrimination against disabled persons;
- to promote the equalisation of opportunities for disabled persons;
- to take such steps as it considers appropriate with a view to encouraging good practice in the treatment of disabled persons; and
- to keep under review the working of the Disability Discrimination Act 1995 and the Disability Rights Commission Act 1999.

The DRC 1999 gives the Commission an extensive role and numerous powers. It can be anticipated that in the years to come one of the key roles of the Commission will be in the promotion of litigation, which will push forward the law on disability discrimination.

STRATEGIC CONSIDERATIONS

In practical terms the practitioner in this field, like the employer, whilst having to possess a degree of familiarity with all three statutes and the various *Codes, Guidance* and secondary legislation, will principally be concerned with the employment provisions of the Disability Discrimination Act 1995 and proceedings within the employment tribunal.

This state of affairs exists for a number of reasons. Whilst many disabled people may be aggrieved that they receive "rough treatment" from a particular service provider, few will wish to take civil proceedings where no Legal Aid is available, for a modest amount of compensation. Compensation for Part III claims in the county court will in most cases be limited to injury to feelings. The loss of a job or persistent discrimination in the every day environment of the workplace is a different matter.

The potential for claims to be brought under the Human Rights Act 1998 undoubtedly exists, but it might be postulated that relatively few claims will be brought at first due to a combination of reasons, such as funding problems and the unfamiliarity of judges and lawyers with human rights concepts. The HRA 1998 will lead to the advancement of disabled rights in general, as opposed to redress in the case of the individual. This will be dependant upon the assertion of positive obligations inherent in particular rights, a concept that the legal system in this country might be slow to accept.

So in day-to-day legal practice the disability discrimination lawyer will also be an employment lawyer. The added value that knowledge of the other discrimination provisions brings will be useful, and might lead to a fresh perspective being brought to bear on a particular case.

The legal framework in relation to disability discrimination is, at the time of printing, in a state of flux. This is because it remains uncertain whether or not the HRA 1998 can be used in a radical way to go beyond the limitations of the DDA 1995 in order to give additional rights to disabled people. It remains uncertain how the existence of the HRA 1998 will interact with the provisions of the DDA 1995.

Part III of the DDA 1995 might be viewed as a relative failure in terms of preventing discrimination in relation to disabled people, as it seems to have resulted in a tiny number of cases being brought. Most of these cases on an individual basis would fall to be considered in the Small Claims Track and would be worth relatively little in terms of compensation.

But the legal framework cannot be viewed in isolation. There is scope to use the provisions that currently exist in an imaginative way. The use of those provisions in such a way is largely dependent on the will of disabled people and in particular the increasingly vocal civil rights lobby amongst disabled people. The establishment of the Disability Rights Commission by the DRCA 1999 may also have established a powerful engine, which in years to come will take a leading role in the advancement of test cases.

One example of the way provisions currently in existence could be used far more effectively, would be where a significant number of disabled people have suffered discrimination from a provider of services. Instead of bringing small claims in isolation, it would be possible using the provisions of part 19 of the Civil Procedure Rules to have a Group Litigation Order made for example, with favourable provisions for case management, judicial expertise and costs. But this would require a pro-active approach from disabled people or their lobbying organisations which to date has not been forthcoming.

SUMMARY

- There are three principal statutes the DDA 1995, the HRA 1998 and the DRCA 1999 that form the legal framework within which claims can be made.
- The principal statute for the purpose of litigation is the DDA 1995.Regard should be had to the wealth of secondary legislation, *Codes* and *Guidance* that have been made under the DDA 1995.
- The ambit of the HRA 1998 is unclear and its ramifications for disability discrimination litigation are uncertain.
- The Disability Rights Commission could become a major force in using litigation to push forward the boundaries of the law.

CHAPTER TWO
DEFINING DISABILITY

SYNOPSIS

In disability discrimination litigation, disabled people bring claims. But who counts as disabled? Blind people and those in wheelchairs are only the most obvious example of those disabled people who are entitled to bring a claim. The DDA 1995 has a definition of whom is disabled, which whilst simple in concept has created complications if not confusion in practice.

THE CONCEPTS

A person in a wheelchair or with a white stick would obviously be seen to be disabled. In the context of the disability discrimination legislation that everyday perception of disability will also accord with the definition of disability contained within the DDA 1995. But other cases will not be so clear-cut. Questions of fact and degree will be have to be examined, in order to determine whether, for example a 55 year old man with a back complaint is simply a man with a bad back, or a man with a bad back with a sufficient degree of disability to afford him rights against discrimination as a disabled person.

Conversely the first line of attack against a claim for disability discrimination, for a respondent or defendant, will be to challenge whether the applicant or claimant is in fact disabled within the meaning of the DDA 1995.

THE DEFINITION WITHIN THE DISABILITY DISCRIMINATION ACT 1995

Only disabled persons can bring a claim under the DDA 1995. Section 1 of the DDA 1995 provides:

> (1) Subject to the provisions of Schedule 1, a person has a disability for the purposes of this Act if he has a physical or mental impairment which has a substantial and long-term adverse effect on his ability to carry out normal day-to-day activities.

It should be noted that people who have had such disabilities in the past would also attract the protection of the Act, by virtue of section 2, which extends the ambit of disability to include past disabilities (Section 2 DDA 1995). Schedule 1 of the DDA 1995 provides more detail to flesh out the terms of section 1.

IMPAIRMENT

- Mental impairment includes an impairment resulting from or consisting of mental illness only if the illness is clinically well recognised.
- Regulations can prescribe conditions which will be treated as amounting to or not amounting to an impairment.

LONG-TERM EFFECTS

- A long-term effect is one which has lasted at least twelve months, or is likely to last twelve months, or is likely to last the rest of the life of the person affected.
- If an impairment ceases to have a substantial adverse effect, it is to be treated as continuing, if the effect is likely to recur.
- Regulations may prescribe that the likelihood of recurrence is to be disregarded or when an effect is to be treated as a long-term effect or when an otherwise long-term effect should be disregarded.

SEVERE DISFIGUREMENT

- A severe disfigurement is to be treated as having a substantial adverse effect on the ability of a person to carry out day-to-day activities.

- Regulations can prescribed when severe disfigurements would not have that effect, including deliberately acquired disfigurements.

NORMAL DAY-TO-DAY ACTIVITIES

- For an impairment to affect day-to-day activities it must affect:
  - mobility
  - manual dexterity
  - physical co-ordination
  - continence
  - ability to lift, carry or move everyday objects
  - speech, hearing or eyesight
  - memory or ability to concentrate, learn or understand
  - perception of the risk of physical danger
- Regulations may prescribe circumstances in which an impairment which does not have one of these effects is to be treated as so doing or when an impairment which does, is to be treated as not doing so.

SUBSTANTIAL ADVERSE EFFECTS

- Regulations may prescribe for an effect of a prescribed kind to be treated as a substantial adverse effect or not.

EFFECT OF MEDICAL TREATMENT

- If measures are taken to treat or correct an impairment which prevent it from having what would otherwise be a substantial adverse effect, it is to be treated as so having that substantial adverse effect.
- Measures taken can include but are not limited to medical treatment and the use of a prosthesis.
- This provision does not apply to vision, which can be corrected by spectacles or contact lenses, or other circumstances prescribed by regulations.

PROGRESSIVE CONDITIONS

- If a person has a progressive condition, such as cancer, MS, muscular dystrophy or HIV, and has an impairment affecting normal day-to-day activities, but which is not (yet) a substantial adverse effect, he is deemed to have impairment with a substantial adverse effect if the condition is likely to result in such an impairment.

THE DISABILITY DISCRIMINATION (MEANING OF DISABILITY) REGULATIONS 1996

It can be seen that Schedule 1 of the DDA 1995 provides for secondary legislation to prescribe certain effects or conditions as having a deemed status. The relevant regulations brought into force in respect of this provision are the Disability Discrimination (Meaning of Disability) Regulations 1996 (SI 1996/1455). These provide:

- Addictions to alcohol, nicotine or other substances than medically prescribed drugs do not amount to impairments for the purposes of the DDA 1995.
- Tendencies to set fires, steal, physically or sexually abuse other persons, exhibitionism and voyeurism are also not to be treated as impairments.
- Seasonal allergic rhinitis in isolation cannot amount to an impairment.
- A tattoo or a piercing of the body for decorative or other non-medical purposes is not to be treated as a severe disfigurement amounting to an impairment within the DDA 1995.
- Children under six years who have impairments which do not (yet) affect in a long term and substantially adverse way their day-to-day activities will be deemed to have such impairments if the impairment would normally have that effect on people over the age of six.

DETERMINING DISABILITY: GUIDANCE

Section 3 of the DDA 1995 provides for the Secretary of State to issue *Guidance* about the matters to be taken into account, when determining:

- Whether an impairment has a substantial adverse effect on a person's ability to carry out normal day-to-day activities;
- Whether such an impairment has a long-term effect.

This *Guidance* (if relevant) must be taken into account by a tribunal or court when determining whether an impairment has a substantial and long-term adverse effect on a person's ability to carry out normal day-to-day activities (Section 3(3) DDA 1995).

The *Guidance* summarises the four criteria for defining someone as disabled within the ambit of the DDA 1995. The person must:

- Have an impairment that is physical or mental.
- The impairment must have substantial effects.
- These effects must be long term.
- The long-term substantial effects must be adverse effects on normal day-to-day activities.

The *Guidance* then focuses on the meaning to be attached to the terms, substantial, long term and normal day-to-day activities.

A substantial effect is defined as one which is more than minor or trivial. The *Guidance* makes the points that impairment might not have a substantial adverse effect in relation to day-to-day activities with each activity viewed in isolation, but it can have a cumulative effect, which will satisfy the description "substantial" (*Guidance* A4).

The *Guidance* further goes onto describe how an effect can be long term, though a condition can improve or an adverse effect come and go. The provisions, which deal with the likelihood of recurrence and the discounting of the ameliorative effects of medical treatment, are further defined.

The final section of the *Guidance* goes onto consider the words "substantial adverse" effect in the context of day-to-day activities. For example, in terms of mobility, inability to go out of doors unaccompanied is postulated to amount to a substantial adverse effect, whilst inability to travel in a car for more than two hours without discomfort would not be a substantial adverse effect (*Guidance* C14).

THE CASE LAW

The wealth of reference material which exists dealing with the definition of disability, should render it a simple question of fact as to whether someone satisfies the criteria or not. Nonetheless considerable problems can arise when considering this question and in particular if the entitlement of someone to bring a DDA claim is challenged, what evidence needs to be adduced to substantiate a claim that the applicant or claimant falls within the definition.

In the employment context two decisions are of particular significance in terms of the correct approach to be adopted when resolving this question.

In the case of *Goodwin* v *The Patent Office* [1999] IRLR 4, the employment appeal tribunal was expressly asked to give guidance as to how employment tribunals should approach the definition of disability flowing from section 1, DDA 1995. The employment appeal tribunal decided:

- The tribunal should look carefully at what the parties have said in the originating application and response to ensure that the real questions in issue have been identified.
- In many cases it will be good practice to make standard directions to clarify the issues or to arrange a directions hearing.
- If the parties wish to present expert evidence to assist the tribunal, it is undesirable that such evidence should be given without proper advance notice to the other party and the early provision of any expert report to be referred to.
- The tribunal has an interventionist role in relation to equal value claims and the model set out in Schedule 2 of the procedural rules might be thought a good model for disability cases.
- A purposive approach to construction of the legislation should be adopted.

Reference should always be made explicitly to any relevant provision of the *Guidance* or *Code* which has been taken into account when reaching the Tribunal's decision.

- The tribunal must look at the evidence by reference to the four criteria in section 1(1) but must also be aware of the risk of dis-aggregation and should not take its eye off the whole picture. The emphasis is on what a person cannot do, rather than what they can do.

The case of *Vicary* v *British Telecommunications plc* [1999] IRLR 680 adds a further dimension to the issue as to how the issue of disability should be approached. In that case, the applicant was found as a fact by the tribunal to be unable (amongst other things) to prepare vegetables, manually open jars, carry baskets of washing, read without resting the book, do heavy shopping, do any DIY tasks, file her nails, iron, shake quilts, groom animals, knit, sew and use scissors. The tribunal went onto hold that she was not disabled within the meaning of the Act! Overturning the decision on appeal the employment appeal tribunal held:

- The *Guidance* is only of assistance in marginal cases. The tribunal had no need to refer to the *Guidance* when they properly understood that substantial means more than minor or trivial.
- The medical evidence of the respondent's occupational health adviser was largely irrelevant, in that it is not for a doctor to express an opinion as to what is a normal day-to-day activity or whether the impairments found proved were to be regarded as substantial. These are matters for the tribunal.
- An expert is entitled to put forward observations of the applicant carrying out day-to-day activities and to comment on the ease or otherwise with which the functions were being performed.
- Only a small proportion of the disabled community are visibly disabled. It is important that tribunals do not approach this question with a stereotypical attitude.

STRATEGIC CONSIDERATIONS

The issue of disability and who is disabled is one that has proved complicated in a number of ways. That portion of the disabled community which has plain and obvious disability, such as blindness or paraplegia, will obviously fall within the ambit of the definition considered above and will be afforded the protection of the DDA 1995. But those who suffer, for example, from chronic fatigue syndrome, or a troublesome back condition, will not obviously fall within the ambit of the DDA 1995. If they contend that they have been discriminated against the first issue that falls to be considered is whether or not they are in fact disabled.

This question has to be answered by considering the criteria which apply, in the statute, the regulations and the *Guidance*. Once the criteria have been established, it then falls to be a matter of evidence as to whether or not someone is disabled within the ambit of the statute and consequently it is a question of fact for a court or tribunal to determine this question on the evidence.

The most valuable or indeed essential form of evidence is medical evidence, preferably from a Consultant in an appropriate discipline which establishes the disability. At a pinch, a report from a General Practitioner might suffice. This will undoubtedly be supplemented by lay evidence from the disabled person himself or herself, setting out their condition and the effect it has on them. Corroborating evidence from family members or from anyone who has the opportunity to observe the disabled person on a day-to-day basis is also relevant and admissible.

In disability discrimination cases, many tribunals now take as a preliminary point the issue as to whether the applicant is a disabled person within the ambit and meaning of the DDA 1995. This often presents an opportunity for the respondent to a claim to have it dismissed at an early stage. Accordingly even if the tribunal does not make an order of its own motion, this is a point which a respondent in a proper case may well wish to take and should apply for appropriate directions.

It also presents the applicant with something of a "Morton's fork" argument to use at the hearing of a complaint, in that the respondent may well argue that the applicant was not disabled within the meaning of the Act, but will then be in some difficulty in arguing, should a tribunal decide otherwise, that, for example reasonable steps in accordance with a section 6 duty have been taken.

The crucial point for both applicant and respondent is to ensure that appropriate evidence is available to put before the tribunal. This will consist largely of medical evidence, which might be obtained on a joint basis. It should be noted that it is not the role of the expert to make conclusions on points which are properly to be left for the tribunal, such as whether or not the applicant's condition falls within the ambit and meaning of disabled within the definition of the DDA 1995.

It may well be necessary for the medical experts to attend for cross-examination, but by borrowing techniques from the civil jurisdiction for use employment cases, it may be possible for written questions to obviate the need for attendance of the witness at trial.

In the civil jurisdiction, there is of course provision in part 35 of the Civil Procedure Rules for a single expert to be appointed by the court to assist on the determination of the issue of disability. The normal rules would apply and unless the report proved particularly obscure or contentious, would be adduced in written form in court.

SUMMARY

- The concept of a disability and who is entitled to the protection of the DDA 1995 should be a simple one.
- The application of the concept has proved troublesome in practice.
- Regard should be had to the provisions of the statute, the regulations and the *Guidance* in determining whether a person falls within the definition of disability contained in the DDA 1995.
- The issue of disability will largely turn on the available medical evidence, supplemented by lay evidence.
- A respondent or defendant can obtain an advantage by having the issue of disability and a person's entitlement to bring a claim determined as a preliminary issue.

CHAPTER THREE
THE JURISDICTION OF THE EMPLOYMENT TRIBUNAL

SYNOPSIS

The majority of claims for disability discrimination which have been brought to date, arise from the context of the employment provisions of the DDA 1995. This chapter considers the jurisdiction of the employment tribunal that is the forum for such claims.

THE CONCEPTS

A fundamental division in the DDA 1995 exists between claims arising out of the employment context and claims arising out of the provision of goods and services. This division is expressed in the Act by claims that arise out of the employment context being brought under Part II of the DDA 1995 in the employment tribunal and claims for discrimination in the provision of goods and services, under Part III of the DDA 1995 in the county court.

THE JURISDICTION OF THE EMPLOYMENT TRIBUNAL

The employment tribunal is given jurisdiction to entertain disability discrimination claims by section 8 of the DDA 1995:

(1) A complaint by any person that another person –
  (a) has discriminated against him in a way which is unlawful under this Part, or
  (b) is, by virtue of section 57 or 58, to be treated as having discriminated against him in such a way,

may be presented to an employment tribunal.

Further provisions in Part I of Schedule 3 deal with procedure (section 8 (8) DDA 1995). Part I of Schedule 3 is concerned to provide for conciliation, to restrict proceedings by excluding any other criminal or civil liability (except through judicial review) and to provide time limits for the bringing of a complaint.

TIME LIMITS FOR PRESENTING A COMPLAINT

Paragraph 3 of Part I of Schedule 3 provides:

> (1) An employment tribunal shall not consider a complaint under section 8 unless it is presented before the end of the period of three months beginning when the act complained or was done.
>
> (2) A tribunal may consider any such complaint which is out of time if, in all the circumstances of the case, it considers that it is just and equitable to do so.
>
> (3) For the purposes of sub-paragraph (1) –
> (a) where an unlawful act of discrimination is attributable to a term in a contract, that act is to be treated as extending throughout the duration of the contract;
> (b) any act extending over a period shall be treated as done at the end of that period; and
> (c) a deliberate omission shall be treated as done when the person in question decided upon it.
>
> 4) In the absence of evidence establishing the contrary, a person shall be taken for the purposes of this paragraph to decide upon an omission –
> (a) when he does an act inconsistent with doing the omitted act; or
> (b) if he has done no such inconsistent act, when the period expires within which he might reasonably have been expected to do the omitted act if it was to be done.

THE SMALL BUSINESS EXEMPTION

It should be noted that the provisions of the DDA 1995 do not (as yet) provide protection to all disabled employees or putative employees. This is because of the small business exemption contained in section 7 of the DDA 1995, as modified by the Disability Discrimination (Exemption for Small Employers) Order 1998 (SI 1998/2618). This provides that Part II does not apply to an employer who has fewer than 15 employees.

This provision was examined in the case of *Hardie* v *CD Northern Limited* [2000] IRLR 87. In this case an issue arose as to whether or not an employer had less than the then limit of 20 employees. The tribunal found that the employer had 19 employees and dismissed the application. There were associated companies as part of a larger corporate structure which did have more employees, but the employment appeal tribunal rejected an appeal:

- There was no scope for importing into the DDA 1995 any concept of an "associated" employer.
- There was no reason to lift the corporate veil in circumstances where the simple fact of the corporate structure and contract of employment indicated there was but one employer.

This falls to be contrasted with the decision of the employment appeal tribunal in *Taylor* v *Lifesign Ltd (in liquidation)*(2000) *New Law Digest* 23rd March, a case where an employer had less than 20 employees but was supplied with a sales force of some 60 sales representatives by a third party. This brought into consideration issues under section 12(3) DDA 1995, which required remission to the tribunal to consider the evidence on whether the existence of this sales force affected the exemption.

OTHER EXEMPTIONS FROM THE PROVISIONS OF PART II

Small businesses are not the only employers who enjoy an exemption from the employment provisions of the DDA 1995. According to section 64(5) to 64(7), Part II will not apply to members of the MOD police, British Transport police, Royal Parks Constabulary, UK Atomic Energy Authority Constabulary, prison officers, fire fighters and members of the armed services.

THE AMBIT OF DISCRIMINATION

The opening section of Part II (section 4 DDA 1995) sets out in simple terms what is prohibited on the part of an employer. Subsection (1) is concerned with putative employees:

> (1) It is unlawful for an employer to discriminate against a disabled person –
> (a) in the arrangements which he makes for the purpose of determining to whom he should offer employment;
> (b) in the terms on which he offers that person employment; or

(c) by refusing to offer, or deliberately not offering, him employment.

Subsection (2) is directed at protecting disabled people who are already employed by the employer:

(2) It is unlawful for an employer to discriminate against a disabled person whom he employs –
(a) in the terms of employment which he affords him;
(b) in the opportunities which he affords him for promotion, a transfer, training or receiving any other benefit;
(c) by refusing to afford him, or deliberately not affording him, any such opportunity; or
(d) by dismissing him, or subjecting him to any other detriment.

The subject of benefits is further defined within the section (by 4(3)-(4), DDA 1995) and expressly stated to include facilities and services. A territorial limit is placed on the section, which only applies to employment at an establishment in Great Britain.

THE MEANING OF DISCRIMINATION

Having defined how discrimination can take place in the employment context, the question then arises, as to what constitutes discrimination? It should be noted at this point that discrimination as defined in the DDA 1995, is very different from the definitions of discrimination to be found in the Sex Discrimination Act 1975 or the Race Relations Act 1976. In essence discrimination can take place in two ways as defined by section 5 of the DDA 1995. The first of these is discrimination by way of less favourable treatment which is unjustified:

(1) For the purposes of this Part, an employer discriminates against a disabled person if –
(a) for a reason which relates to the disabled person's disability he treats him less favourably than he treats or would treat others to whom that reason does not or would not apply; and
(b) he cannot show that the treatment in question is justified.

This could be described as direct discrimination. It should be noted that it is perfectly possible to treat a disabled person less favourably, without that treatment constituting discrimination provided it can be justified.

The second form of discrimination contemplated by the DDA 1995 is the failure to comply with a section 6 duty:

> (2) For the purposes of this Part an employer also discriminates against a disabled person if –
> (a) he fails to comply with a section 6 duty imposed on him in relation to the disabled person; and
> (b) he cannot show that his failure to comply with duty is justified.

A section 6 duty is one to take reasonable steps to prevent any arrangements made by or on behalf of the employer or any physical features of premises occupied by the employer, from placing a disabled person at a substantial disadvantage in comparison with persons who are not disabled. This duty to take reasonable steps is commonly referred to as the duty to make "reasonable adjustments".

It should again be noted that a failure to take reasonable steps does not automatically constitute discrimination, provided that the failure can be justified.

THE DISABILITY DISCRIMINATION (QUESTIONS AND REPLIES) ORDER 1996, SI 1996/2793

The DDA 1995, by section 56, makes provision for the service of a questionnaire upon an alleged discriminator by the complainant in the context of employment provisions, in order to assist the complainant in deciding whether to make a complaint against the potential discriminator and to formulate and present his case in an effective manner. The recipient of such a questionnaire cannot be compelled to answer it and failure to do so does not raise any presumption of discrimination. But the questionnaire or the answers to it can have a real role to play in tribunal proceedings. The DDA 1995 provides:

> (2) Where the complainant questions the respondent in accordance with forms prescribed by an order under subsection (2) –
> (a) the question, and any reply by the respondent (whether in accordance with such an order or not) shall be admissible as evidence in any proceedings under Part II;
> (b) if it appears to the tribunal in any such proceedings –
> (i) that the respondent deliberately, and without reasonable excuse, omitted to reply within a reasonable period, or

(ii) that the respondent's reply is evasive or equivocal, it may draw any inference which it considers it just and equitable to draw, including an inference that the respondent has contravened a provision of Part II.

STRATEGIC CONSIDERATIONS

A lawyer contemplating a claim for disability discrimination will often wish to couple this with perhaps a claim for unfair dismissal or raise issues of constructive dismissal. Pure disability discrimination cases will be relatively rare. It follows that a broad knowledge of employment law is a necessary adjunct to expertise in the area of disability discrimination.

Time limits for bringing disability discrimination claims are tight. Three months is the relevant limitation period and it follows that a degree of expedition will often be required when first instructed in such a case. The time limit can be extended and the tribunal has a broad discretion in which to do so. It does so on the basis of whether it is just and equitable to do so, as between the applicant and the respondent. Case law which has been decided in the context of the time limits in sex and race discrimination cases will undoubtedly be of significance in relation to attempts to extend the time limit in disability cases. There are likely to be differences in approach and peculiar factors which relate to disability cases, but this body of authority will provide a starting point.

Knowledge of the time limits and correct identification of the limitation period is the pre-requisite for any lawyer undertaking work in this area, for professional indemnity purposes if nothing else. When an extension of the time limit needs to be sought, powerful arguments for its extension can often be made arising from the nature of the disabled person's disability or their difficulties in obtaining legal advice. The test of "just and equitable" is far easier to satisfy than the test of "not reasonably practicable", which applies in the context of other employment statutes.

It should be noted that a particular employer might very well fall to be exempt from the provisions of the DDA 1995 depending on the size of his establishment and also of course, on who is the employer. Certain organisations such as the armed forces will also have an exemption. The exemptions for certain employers based on size and also in relation to the nature of the organisation, which preclude disabled people from bringing claims for what might be otherwise clear cut discrimination are vulnerable to attack for incompatibility with the European Convention on Human Rights. This may not be of great comfort to a private individual wishing to sue a private sector employer, but could constitute one of the test cases which the coming into force of the HRA 1998 allows.

The DDA 1995 draws a precise definition of discrimination based on two concepts: less favourable treatment; and a failure to take reasonable steps to comply with duties laid on an employer or prospective employer. This dichotomy is unique to the DDA 1995 and does not reflect the dichotomy present in other discrimination statutes between direct and indirect discrimination. It will be vital when advising a disabled person to consider whether the acts or omissions they complain of fall within one or other or both of these distinct categories of discrimination.

The use of a questionnaire is available to all potential applicants but is frequently neglected. In reality every case involving disability discrimination should make use of a questionnaire, which can be sent to the respondent and will often be answered by the respondent, before he takes recourse to his lawyers. If it is not answered, or answered after a significant delay, this in itself can be used as ammunition against the respondent at any hearing.

Every complainant should use the questionnaire procedure in a disability discrimination case and every respondent to such a questionnaire, should take legal advice before answering it, treating the questionnaire as a letter before action, as in many cases it will be the precursor to such a letter. The answers or failure to give answers can prove very significant in a disability discrimination case. At the very least, delay can be used in cross-examination to expose the lack of regard which a particular respondent has to disabled issues.

SUMMARY

- The majority of disability discrimination litigation in this country will take place within the context of the employment tribunal.
- It is essential that disability discrimination lawyers have a broad knowledge of employment law, as it will be rare for disability discrimination claims to be brought in isolation to other claims, such as unfair dismissal.
- The time limits which apply in tribunal proceedings are particularly tight and regard must be had to the basis upon which the limit can be extended.

- Certain employers enjoy an exemption from the DDA 1995 due to their size or nature. These exemptions are open to challenge due to the coming into force of the HRA 1998.
- It is essential to distinguish whether a disabled person's complaint is one of less favourable treatment or a failure to comply with a section 6 duty or both.

CHAPTER FOUR
LESS FAVOURABLE TREATMENT IN THE WORKPLACE

SYNOPSIS

Disability discrimination in the employment context has two branches. A person can be discriminated against by being treated less favourably than others or by the failure of an employer to comply with a section 6 duty which the DDA 1995 places upon him. This chapter explores the concept of less favourable treatment and what it means in practice.

THE CONCEPTS

Less favourable treatment or direct discrimination as it is often called, is theoretically a straightforward concept. Yet in the early years of the operation of the DDA 1995 it has caused considerable problems in practice and has also generated the first Court of Appeal decision on the provisions of the DDA 1995.

THE CONCEPT OF LESS FAVOURABLE TREATMENT

The wording of section 5(1) reads:

> (1) For the purposes of this Part, an employer discriminates against a disabled person if –
> (a) for a reason which relates to the disabled person's disability he treats him less favourably than he treats or would treat others to whom that reason does not or would not apply; and

(b) he cannot show that the treatment in question is justified.

The section requires a number of distinct elements to be proved for discrimination to be established. There must be:

- a causal link between treatment and a reason related to a disabled person's disability;
- less favourable treatment compared to others to whom the disability related reason does not apply;
- no justification for the less favourable treatment.

If these three elements are met, then a finding of discrimination can be made.

The case of *British Sugar plc* v *Kirker* [1998] IRLR 624 is authority for the proposition that treatment before the coming into force of the DDA 1995 can be considered relevant in determining whether less favourable treatment has occurred under the provisions of the DDA 1995.

THE REASON FOR THE TREATMENT MUST BE RELATED TO THE DISABILITY

The wording of section 5(1), with the requirement that less favourable treatment must be related to the disability, requires a causal link to be established between a disabled person's disability and what may appear to be unjustified less favourable treatment. It is open to a tribunal to find less favourable treatment but that this was for a non-disability related reason.

This is a straightforward question of fact, illustrated in the case of *Murphy* v *Sheffield Hallam University*, a decision of the employment appeal tribunal. In that case a deaf person who applied for a job with the respondent, was found to have been discriminated against, in that despite his intimation of his disability, no arrangements were made for an interpreter to be initially present at his interview. However his failure to obtain the job, after an adjourned interview, was found on the facts to be due to the respondent appointing a person they perceived to be the best man for the job.

A further point which requires consideration, is whether an employer who claims to be ignorant of a disabled person's disability, can establish that such ignorance precludes any less favourable treatment being for a reason related to a disability, as the employer lacked the necessary knowledge to discriminate. This question has resulted in a division of opinion in the employment appeal tribunal.

In the case of *O'Neill* v *Symm & Co Ltd* [1998] IRLR 233, the applicant alleged that she suffered from ME or Chronic Fatigue Syndrome (CFS) and was dismissed due to her high level of absence. The employment appeal tribunal held:

CFS is not a generic condition or a category of disability that necessarily falls within the ambit of the DDA 1995.

- The use of the word reason in section 5(1) connotes that a knowledge is required of the matter that is material.
- What is material to discrimination on the ground of disability is disability and not merely one or other equivocal symptom, just as what is material in pregnancy cases is knowledge of the pregnancy.

Conversely in the case of *HJ Heinz Co Ltd* v *Kenrick* [2000] IRLR 144 a rather different approach was taken. In that case an applicant suffered from chronic fatigue syndrome (CFS) which was accepted in the case to be a disability. At the time of his dismissal respondent knew of the symptoms of the condition, but not its name. The employment appeal tribunal went on to consider *O'Neill*:

- The employment appeal tribunal would hesitate before adopting the view that there cannot be less favourable treatment before an employer has knowledge of the disability or the material features of it.
- There is no requirement in section 5(1) that the relationship between the disability and the treatment should be adjudged subjectively through the eyes of the employer.
- The applicable test should be the objective one of whether the relationship exists, not whether the employer knew of it.
- Unless the test is objective, cases with credible and honest, yet ignorant and obtuse employers who fail to recognise or acknowledge the obvious will create difficulties.

THE OTHERS TO WHOM THAT REASON DOES NOT OR WOULD NOT APPLY

The requirement that less favourable treatment is to be assessed against the treatment afforded to other persons, to whom disability related reasons do not apply imports into disability discrimination law the concept of a comparator, a concept easily recognisable in other branches of discrimination law.

But this created a problem when further consideration was given to who the comparator was to be? Was it a simply a person without a disability or a person with the same characteristics as a disabled person without a disability?

THE PROVISIONS OF THE CODE OF PRACTICE

The *Code of Practice* relevant to employment matters has remarkably little to say on the matter of the comparator. In the relevant provisions (paras 4.2 to 4.3) two simple examples are drawn, before the *Code* goes on to consider the issue of reasonable adjustments. But the comparator can be absolutely crucial in determining whether discrimination has taken place.

The decision of the Court of Appeal in *Clark* v *TDG Ltd t/a Novacold*

The problem was firmly grasped by the Court of Appeal in the case of *Clark* v *TDG Ltd t/a Novacold* [1999] IRLR 318. In that case an applicant who sustained a back injury at work had an extended period of sick leave and was ultimately dismissed. At first instance the tribunal held that there was no less favourable treatment, in that the applicant had been treated the same way as other employees would have been who were off work for a similar length of time but for a non-disability related reason. The comparator was thus an employee who had extensive time off work but was not disabled.

The Court of Appeal held that this was not the test:

- The test of less favourable treatment is based on the reason for the treatment of the disabled person and not on the fact of his disability.
- It does not turn on a like for like comparison of the treatment of the disabled person and of others in similar circumstances.
- It is inappropriate to make a comparison of the cases in the same way as in the Sex Discrimination and Race Relations Acts.
- The Disability Discrimination Act does not contain an express provision requiring a comparison of the cases of different persons in the same or not materially different circumstances. The statutory focus is narrower.
- A specific example drawn from the text of the judgment (ibid at page 324) neatly illustrates the point. A cafe owner puts up a sign saying no dogs allowed. A blind person with a guide dog and a sighted person with their pet dog are both refused admission. On the analysis of the tribunal, there would be no discrimination as all dog owners have been

treated equally. On the test adopted by the Court of Appeal, the blind person has been refused admission, his treatment has been less favourable as compared to that of sighted persons without dogs and accordingly there has been less favourable treatment.

THE CONCEPT OF JUSTIFICATION

Justification is further defined in the following way:

> (3) Subject to subsection (5) for the purposes of subsection (1) treatment is justified if, but only if, the reason for it is both material to the circumstances of the particular case and substantial.

A further provision, which is worded in a circuitous and obscure manner, is contained in a later subsection of section 5:

> (5) If, in a case falling within sub-section (1), the employer is under a section 6 duty in relation to the disabled person but fails without justification to comply with that duty, his treatment of that person cannot be justified under subsection (3) unless it would have been justified even if he had complied with the section 6 duty.

This provision would appear to mean that if a section 6 duty has been not complied with and there is no justification for that, so discrimination is found. However, this precludes an argument of justification being raised in relation to less favourable treatment unless even supposing the section 6 duty had been complied with, there would still have been justification for less favourable treatment.

The case of *Baynton* v *Saurus General Engineers Ltd* [1999] IRLR 604 provides some guidance on the interrelationship between the defence of justification less favourable treatment and a failure to discharge section 6 duties. In that case the employment appeal tribunal held that the question of a section 6 duty is not irrelevant to justification on a complaint of less favourable treatment in that it is necessary for the respondent to show for the purpose of establishing the requirements of section 5(3) that the reason for dismissal was material to the circumstances of the case and substantial and that the respondent has not without justification failed to comply with any duty under section 6.

Regard should also be had to the provisions of the Disability Discrimination (Employment) Regulations 1996 SI 1996 No 1456, which are made under

Part II of the DDA 1995 and provide prescribed instances of when less favourable treatment will be justified.

STRATEGIC CONSIDERATIONS

Discrimination through less favourable treatment has a number of definitional elements. There must be less favourable treatment, there must be a causal link between this and the disabled person's disability and there must be no justification for the treatment. In terms of defending a claim, the definitional elements of less favourable treatment can form a number of hurdles for the complainant to cross. The first element is to establish less favourable treatment. There is no room in the definition for arguments that treatment is "separate but equal". It is possible for arguments to be raised that a particular instance of treatment was not, as a matter of fact, less favourable but neutral or even beneficial (in a way that was not appreciated by the disabled person). But these are not arguments, which usually find favour with a tribunal, which takes a broad view of what constitutes less favourable treatment. Arguments which are more likely to succeed are that the treatment was for some reason unconnected to the person's disability: and any number of circumstances can be advanced to establish alternative reasons for treatment.

The focus of the definition of direct discrimination is materially different from that which exists in sex and race discrimination cases, as the position of the comparator, assumes a much less significant role. The focus is on less favourable treatment causally related to the disability, with the shadowy figure of the comparator, a notionally non-disabled or even differently disabled, figure in the background. The decision in the case of *Clark* v *TDG t/a Novacold* supra is welcome in that it has clarified the basis on which tribunals should approach the question of less favourable treatment. The use of a comparator with additional qualities or in specific circumstances would undoubtedly have narrowed the ambit of discriminatory treatment.It should also be noted that the issue as to whether less favourable treatment was for a reason related to disability is ultimately a question of fact for the tribunal having heard the evidence. On this basis it is open to the tribunal to accept evidence that whatever the initial reading of a situation might suggest, the reason for a particular appointment or treatment was not related to disability. In other words the defence exemplified by the cliche, that "the best man got the job."

A further question is whether or not it is open to a respondent to claim lack of knowledge of a person's disability as precluding the causal link being made. The question then falls to be considered, of what the plain and ordinary word "knowledge" connotes. Is it certainty or a degree of appreciation less than certainty? Can a respondent be fixed with constructive or shut eye knowledge? How should the issue of knowledge be approached in the light of the conflicting decisions of the employment appeal tribunal?

Many commentators believe that the decision in the case of *Heinz* should be preferred to that *O'Neill*. But this is by no means clearly the law. It is notable that no specific requirement of knowledge exists in relation to a case of direct discrimination, as is embodied in section 6(6) DDA in relation to section 6 duties. Accordingly a tribunal must be referred to both decisions, and in essence it will be a question of fact as to whether treatment was due to a person's disability or disability related reason applying the simple language of the statute.

Although there is a requirement that the less favourable treatment can only be discriminatory if unjustified, in practical terms, it will be for the respondent to raise any defence of justification and to substantiate this in evidential terms. It should be noted that justification must relate to the particular case, in which it is raised and must be substantial, which in this context means more than trivial or minor. This would seem to permit a respondent to establish a defence to a discrimination claim on a relatively broad basis. The defence of justification is flexible. The *Code* gives various examples when a defence of justification is likely to succeed, such as for example a person suffering from psoriasis, who is refused work as a model (*Code of Practice* para 4.6).

SUMMARY

- Less favourable treatment or direct discrimination is ostensibly the most straightforward of the two types of discrimination the employment provisions of the DDA 1995 contemplates.
- The definition of less favourable treatment contains a number of definitional elements which form hurdles for a complainant to cross.
- Less favourable treatment must have a causal link to a disability related reason, to constitute discrimination.
- The authorities are in conflict as to whether or not knowledge of the disability is required to substantiate the causal link.
- A defence of justification exists which has a low threshold. But reference should be had to the *Code of Practice*, in order to assess whether it is likely to be made out.

CHAPTER FIVE
REASONABLE ADJUSTMENTS BY THE EMPLOYER

SYNOPSIS

Discrimination by way of less favourable treatment is only one way in which discrimination can take place. Discrimination can also take place through the failure of an employer to make adjustments pursuant to a duty imposed on him by section 6 DDA 1995. This concept is innovative, wide ranging and the section 6 duties will often prove to be of more significance than a single instance of less favourable treatment.

THE CONCEPTS

Discrimination by way of less favourable treatment or direct discrimination is only one way in which discrimination can occur within the ambit and meaning of the DDA 1995. A failure to comply with a section 6 duty without justification can also amount to unlawful discrimination.

THE SECTION 6 DUTIES

Section 6 of the DDA 1995 provides as follows:

(1) Where –
(a) any arrangements made by or on behalf of an employer, or
(b) any physical feature of premises occupied by the employer,
place the disabled person concerned at a substantial disadvantage in comparison with persons who are not disabled, it is the duty of the employer to take such steps as it is reasonable, in all the

circumstances of the case, for him to have to take in order the prevent the arrangements or feature having that effect.

(2) Subsection (1)(a) applies only in relation to –
  (a) arrangements for determining to whom employment should be offered;
  (b) any term, condition, or arrangements on which employment, promotion, a transfer, training or any other benefit is offered or afforded.

POTENTIAL REASONABLE STEPS TO TAKE

Subsection 6(3) of the DDA 1995 provides examples of steps an employer might have to take in discharge of the section 6 duties:

- Making adjustments to premises
- Allocating some of the disabled person's duties to another person
- Transferring him to fill an existing vacancy
- Altering his working hours
- Assigning him to a different place of work
- Allowing him to be absent during working hours for rehabilitation, assessment or treatment
- Giving him or arranging for him to be given training
- Acquiring or modifying equipment
- Modifying instructions or reference manuals
- Modifying procedures for testing or assessment
- Providing a reader or interpreter
- Providing supervision

It should be noted that these are only examples and are not prescriptive. Nor are they to be taken as limiting the scope of the duties imposed upon an employer.

WHEN IT WILL BE REASONABLE TO TAKE STEPS

The threshold as to when it will be reasonable to have to take a particular step or steps, is to be assessed in relation to a number of criteria laid down in section 6(4):

- The extent to which taking the step would prevent the effect in question;
- The extent to which it is practicable for the employer to take the step;
- The financial and other costs which would be incurred by the employer in taking the step and the extent to which taking it would disrupt any of his activities;
- The extent of the employer's financial and other resources;
- The availability to the employer of financial or other assistance with respect to taking the step.

The correct approach for an employment tribunal to adopt when considering a complaint under section 5(2) of the DDA 1995 has been laid down by the employment appeal tribunal in the case of *Morse* v *Wiltshire County Council* [1998] IRLR 352. In that case a sequential approach was advocated:

- First a tribunal must decide whether the provisions of section 6(1) and section 6(2) impose a section 6(1) duty in the circumstances of the particular case.
- Secondly if such a duty exists the tribunal must next decide whether the employer has taken such steps as it is reasonable in all the circumstances of the case for him to have to take in order to prevent the feature or arrangements having the effect of placing the disabled person concerned at a substantial disadvantage in comparison with persons who are not disabled.
- The tribunal must inquire whether the employer could reasonably have taken any of the steps in section 6(3). The purpose of this section is to focus the minds of the employer and the tribunal.
- Simultaneously the tribunal must consider the factors set out in section 6(4).
- Only after consideration of all these steps does the tribunal have to consider whether the employer had shown that any failure to comply with the section 6 duty is justified which means deciding whether it has been shown that the reason for the failure is both material to the circumstances of the case and substantial.
- The tribunal must apply an objective test asking whether the employer has taken such steps as are reasonable, whether the failure is justified. The tribunal reaches its own view as to what is reasonable.

The EAT has considered the nature of section 6 duties and their interrelationship with less favourable treatment. In the case of *Morse* v *Wiltshire County Council,* ibid, it also considered that a section 6 duty arises in the case of dismissal, as well as considerations of less favourable treatment.

This suggestion has however been disapproved in the case of *Baynton* v *Saurus Saurus General Engineers Ltd* [1999] IRLR 604. In the case of the *Post Office* v *Jones* [2000] ICR 388 it made the point that section 5(1) and section 5(2) can overlap, with the result that an application can be made under both sections. The reasoning in the case would also seem to indicate that although specific instances may be relied upon in support of a claim of discrimination in the context of a tribunal, the nature of a section 6 duty is a continuing one, which has to be considered afresh at all points through the employment relationship.

In the case of *Kenny* v *Hampshire Constabulary* [1998] IRLR 624 the ambit of section 6 and the relationship between section 5(1) and 5(2) also fell to be considered. A disabled person with cerebral palsy applied for a job but needed assistance to go to the toilet at work. The employment appeal tribunal held:

- A failure on the part of the employer to make an arrangement for the disabled person's personal needs was not a failure to make an adjustment within the ambit of section 6. Section 6 was concerned with job related matters not personal needs.
- An application for Access to Work funding had been made and the job offer had been withdrawn before this was determined. Potentially this fell within section 5(1) and would be remitted to the tribunal.

THE REQUIREMENT OF KNOWLEDGE

By contrast with less favourable treatment, if the decision of the employment appeal tribunal in the case of *Heinz* v *Kenrick* is to be preferred, there is a specific requirement of knowledge to be possessed by the employer that an applicant or employee has a disability before a duty arises. Section 6(6) reads:

> (6) Nothing in this section imposes any duty on an employer in relation to a disabled person if the employer does not know and could not reasonably be expected to know-
> (a) in the case of an applicant or potential applicant, that the disabled person concerned is, or may be, an applicant for the employment; or

(b) in any case, that that person has a disability and is likely to be affected in the way mentioned in subsection (1).

This section has been considered by the employment appeal tribunal in the case of *Ridout* v *T C Group* [1988] IRLR 628 where an applicant for employment with photosensitive epilepsy was interviewed in a brightly lit room. Some disquiet was expressed by the applicant in relation to the lighting, but no steps were taken to alter it. The employment appeal tribunal had to consider the correct approach to interpretation of this section:

- Subsection (6) requires the tribunal to measure the extent of the duty if any against the actual or assumed knowledge of the employer both as to the disability and its likelihood of causing the individual a substantial disadvantage.
- This is a question of fact for the tribunal. The tribunal was entitled to find that no reasonable employer would be expected to know that the arrangements for this interview would substantially disadvantage the applicant.

EXCLUSIONS FROM THE DUTY TO TAKE REASONABLE STEPS

Certain benefits are specifically excluded from the ambit of section 6:

(11)This section does not apply in relation to any benefit under an occupational pension scheme or any other benefit payable in money or money's worth under a scheme or arrangement for the benefit of employees in respect of –
(a) termination of service;
(b) retirement, old age or death;
(c) accident, injury, sickness or invalidity; or
(d) any other prescribed matter.

THE DEFENCE OF JUSTIFICATION

A defence of justification also exists in relation to failure to take steps which it would otherwise be reasonable to take, in the context of compliance with a section 6 duty. Thus section 5 provides:

(2) For the purposes of this Part, an employer also discriminates against a disabled person if-
(a) he fails to comply with a section 6 duty imposed on him in relation to the disabled person; and

(b) he cannot show that his failure to comply with that duty is justified.

(4) For the purposes of subsection (2), failure to comply with a section 6 duty is justified if, but only if, the reason for the failure is both material to the circumstances of the particular case and substantial.

Again regard should also be had to the provisions of the Disability Discrimination (Employment) Regulations 1996 SI 1996/1456.

STRATEGIC CONSIDERATIONS

Section 6 duties are very broad in scope but the limitations inherent in the duties should be considered. Section 6 will not require an employer to provide transport to take a disabled employee to his place of work for example. The wide scope of the duties is qualified by the fact that they relate to employment rather than imposing duties of social welfare on the employer.

When a disability discrimination claim is being considered, consideration must be given to making it plain on the face of the complaint, whether it is brought on the basis of less favourable treatment or for not compliance with a section 6 duty.

The authorities referred to in this chapter, make it plain that a claim can be brought on the basis that the same acts and omissions constitute both less favourable treatment and also a failure to comply with a section 6 duty. The sole exception would appear to be dismissal, although this would not be the case where constructive unfair dismissal was claimed, the operative cause of which was non-compliance with a section 6 duty.

Consideration should also be given to the limitation provision. Isolated acts of less favourable treatment, might well fall foul of the three month time limit and no assistance might be gained from the provisions which provide in certain circumstances an extended time limit. But it would appear that section 6 is a continuing duty and failure to take steps would constitute a continuing breach up until the point where the appropriate steps are taken, if they ever are. In many cases, a continuing breach of the section 6 duty might occur until the date of termination of employment, in a dismissal case.

When considering whether or not a section 6 claim exists, the lawyers should consider as the tribunal will, the checklist established by the employment appeal tribunal in the case of *Morse* v *Wiltshire County Council*. This provides a systematic approach for consideration of the merits of the section 6 claim.

The complainant will have to establish that the job related arrangements place him at a disadvantage, which is more than minor or trivial. It should be noted that the existence of particular arrangements such as a scrutiny of reasons for absence may be neutral in effect, as viewed by the employer, but viewed as adverse management pressure by a disabled person who has a high sickness rate.

Assuming that the arrangements do present such a disadvantage, the duty to take steps only arises when the employer has the requisite degree of knowledge required by section 6(6). This poses a question: what is knowledge? If a disabled person persistently tells an employer that they wish to have a particular adjustment made, due to their disability, but the employer insists that the disabled person undergo a medical examination to establish his disability and the need for the adjustment, does the employer have knowledge when the disabled person tells them of their needs or when they receive a medical report?

This is undoubtedly a question of fact in every case, but it is submitted that the requirement of knowledge is satisfied when the disabled person tells the employer. At that point they have knowledge. Failure to act until in receipt of a medical report could then be excused on the basis of justification, but this interpretation seems to fit more easily with the tenor of the opening paragraphs of the *Code of Practice*.

The obligation to take steps is qualified by the criterion of reasonableness. This is defined in the DDA 1995, by reference to a number of specific criteria. These criteria must be established by evidence or an argument that to take particular steps would have been unreasonable can be attacked if there is no evidence or the evidence tendered is unconvincing.

Justification is again, a flexible concept that can be deployed in many circumstances, as envisioned by the *Code of Practice* (para 4.34).

Section 6 duties can present real problems for employers, who do not have a policy in place for disabled workers, for employers who have managers who display inflexibility, when the essence of section 6 is accommodating the disabled in a flexible way and it is submitted proves to be the more flexible element of a disability discrimination claim.

SUMMARY

- Section 6 duties and their interrelationship with less favourable treatment must be considered carefully in the context of any disability discrimination claim.
- Section 6 duties present a more flexible cause of action for a complainant with potential advantages in terms of limitation.
- The employment appeal tribunal decision of *Morse* v *Wiltshire County Council* should be considered when evaluating any claim for disability discrimination.
- The requirement of knowledge in relation to section 6 duties presents opportunities to an employer to disclaim an obligation to comply with a section 6 duty.
- The defence of justification can be deployed flexibly to argue against a finding of disability discrimination.

CHAPTER SIX
TRADE ORGANISATIONS AND OTHER PROVISIONS

SYNOPSIS

The provisions of Part II of the DDA 1995 do not just apply to the direct employer/employee or putative employer/employee relationship but have application within the wider sphere of employment relationships. Trade organisations as defined by the Act, and contract workers will also fall within its scope.

THE CONCEPTS

Part II of the DDA 1995 also contains a number of other provisions that apply in the context of employment and can form part of proceedings in the employment tribunal. These provisions extend the ambit of protection from discrimination beyond the employer-employee relationship to encompass contract workers and the activities of trade organisations. Part II also makes specific provision for discriminatory advertisements, the difficulties created for disabled people through employers occupying premises they do not own and may not have the power to alter and the provision of occupational pension schemes and insurance services.

THE POSITION OF CONTRACT WORKERS

Section 12 of the DDA 1995 is concerned to prevent discrimination against contract workers. The section provides:

> (1) It is unlawful for a principal in relation to contract work, to discriminate against a disabled person –

(a) in the terms on which he allows him to do that work;
(b) by not allowing him to do it or continue to do it;
(c) in the way he affords him access to any benefits or by refusing or deliberately omitting to afford him access to them; or
(d) by subjecting him to any other detriment.

The section then goes on to import (at 12(3)) into the contract work relationship the discrimination provisions contained in Part II of the DDA 1995, including the concepts of discrimination by less favourable treatment and the section 6 duties.

The protection from discrimination only applies in relation to work undertaken in Great Britain (12(5)) and the section also defines what work falls within the definition of contract work:

- A "principal" means a person ("A") who makes work available for doing by individuals who are employed by another person who supplies them under a contract made with A.
- "Contract work" means work so made available.
- "Contract worker" means any individual who is supplied to the principal under such a contract (12(6)).

These provisions have been the subject of comment in the Court of Appeal in the case of *Tansell* v *Abbey Life Assurance Co Ltd* [2000] IRLR 387. In that case, a computer consultant was employed by a limited company, of which he was the sole shareholder, who contracted with an employment agency, which in turn contracted with the respondent. The Court of Appeal held that despite the length of the contractual chain and the interposition of the employment agency, the respondent was to be regarded as a principal within the meaning of the section and accordingly owed duties under the DDA 1995.

TRADE ORGANISATIONS

What is a trade organisation? The DDA 1995, section 13(4), defines it as:

> ...an organisation of workers, an organisation of employers or any other organisation whose members carry on a particular profession or trade for the purposes for which the organisation exists.

At section 13(1)-(2) the Act goes onto indicate the ambit of activities within which discrimination is declared unlawful:

- The terms on which it is prepared to admit a disabled person to membership of the organisation;
- The refusal or deliberate non-acceptance of the disabled person's application for membership;
- The way in which the disabled person is afforded access to benefits or by refusing or deliberately omitting to afford the disabled person access to them;
- Depriving the disabled person of membership or variation of the terms on which the disabled person is a member;
- The subjection of the disabled person to any other detriment.

The model of discrimination which exists in the employer-employee context, of discrimination by way of less favourable treatment or by a failure to take reasonable steps is applied in the context of trade organisations. This is contained in section 14 DDA 1995, a provision which mirrors its corresponding section, section 5 DDA 1995. However section 6 duties are described as section 15 duties; it should be noted that section 15 differs in wording and scope from section 6.

Section 15 provides:

> (1) Where –
> (a) any arrangements made by or on behalf of a trade organisation, or
> (b) any physical feature of premises occupied by the organisation,
> place the disabled person concerned at a substantial disadvantage in comparison with persons who are not disabled, it is the duty of the organisation to take such steps as it is reasonable, in all the circumstances of the case, for it to have to take in order the prevent the arrangements or feature having that effect.

The section goes onto deal with the criteria that must be considered when deciding whether or not it is reasonable for a particular step to be taken:

- The extent to which taking the step would prevent the effect in question;
- The extent to which it is practicable for the organisation to take the step;

- The financial and other costs which would be incurred by the organisation in taking the step and the extent to which taking it would disrupt any of its activities;
- The extent of the organisation's financial and other resources;
- The availability to the organisation of financial or other assistance with respect to taking the step;
- The requirement of knowledge that is contained in section 6, is also contained in section 15(5).

ADVERTISEMENTS

The DDA 1995 makes, at section 11, a specific but limited provision in relation to adverts (including every form of advertisement or notice, whether to the public or not) which seem to indicate that disabled people in applying for jobs will be discriminated against. The section applies where a number of criteria are satisfied to create a presumption that the disabled person has been discriminated against unless the contrary is proved. The criteria are:

- a disabled person applies for employment with an employer;
- the employer has refused to offer or deliberately not offered the employment to the disabled person;
- the disabled person brings a complaint to the employment tribunal;
- the employer has advertised the employment either before or after the disabled person's application;
- the advertisement indicates or might reasonably be understood to indicate that any application would or might be determined by the successful person not having a disability or the employer's reluctance to undertake action required by section 6.

LEASEHOLD PREMISES

Alterations to premises, perhaps to improve access for disabled persons, are alterations that any number of reasonable employers might wish to make, perhaps in furtherance of a section 6 duty. But if the premises are leasehold, then an employer by reason of the lease might be precluded from making such alterations or may only be able to make them with the consent of the freeholder.

The DDA 1995 contains far-reaching provisions that interfere with the individual's freedom of contract, to permit alterations to be made. Section 16 reads:

> (2) Except to the extent to which it expressly so provides, the lease shall have effect by virtue of this subsection as if it provided –
> (a) for the occupier to be entitled to make the alteration with the written consent of the lessor;
> (b) for the occupier to have to make a written application to the lessor for consent if he wishes to make the alteration;
> (c) if such an application is made, for the lessor not to withhold his consent unreasonably; and
> (d) for the lessor to be entitled to make his consent subject to reasonable conditions.

The DDA 1995 effectively implies into the lease an additional term, permitting alterations which are reasonable. Section 16 is supplemented by the provisions of Part I of Schedule 4 to the DDA 1995. These provisions provide first that constraints which are imposed by the lease are ignored if the employer has made no attempt to obtain permission to alter the premises (Schedule 4 Part 1 para 1) and also a procedure (Schedule 4 Part 1 para 2) by which a reluctant landlord can be joined into any complaint made by a disabled person by the complainant or the occupier. This could ultimately lead to a declaration being made, an order authorising the occupier to make the alteration and the payment of compensation by the freeholder to the disabled person (Schedule 4 Part 1 para 2(6)).

OCCUPATIONAL PENSION SCHEMES

Section 17 of the DDA 1995 provides:

> (1) Every occupational pension scheme shall be taken to include a provision ("a non discrimination rule") –
> (a) relating to the terms on which –
> (i) persons become members of the scheme; and
> (ii) members of the scheme are treated; and
> (b) requiring the trustees or managers of the scheme to refrain from any act or omission which, if done in relation to a person by an employer, would amount to unlawful discrimination against that person for the purposes of this part.

(2) The other provisions of the scheme are to have effect subject to the non-discrimination rule.

INSURANCE SERVICES

Insurance services are also subject to a non-discrimination provision, as the DDA 1995 at section 18 provides:

(1) This section applies where a provider of insurance services ("the insurer") enters into arrangements with an employer under which the employer's employees, or a class of his employees –
  (a) receive insurance services provided by the insurer; or
  (b) are given an opportunity to received such services.

(2) The insurer is to be taken, for the purposes of this Part to discriminate unlawfully against a disabled person who is a relevant employee if he acts in relation to that employee in a way which would be unlawful discrimination for the purposes of Part III if –
  (a) he were providing the services in question to members of the public; and
  (b) the employee was provided with, or was trying to secure the provision of, that service as a member of the public.

Insurance services mean services for the provision of benefits in respect of termination of service, retirement old age and death, accident injury sickness or invalidity or other matters which might be prescribed (section 18(3) DDA 1995).

STRATEGIC CONSIDERATIONS

The DDA 1995 is social legislation and as the Court of Appeal have made clear is to be given a purposive construction. Accordingly the provisions of the DDA 1995 which relate to contract workers, are intended to give the widest possible protection to workers, as distinct from the traditional notion of an employee, and to accommodate the various relationships under which work is carried out in a modern economy, where the traditional employer/employee relationship is on the wane. The case of *Tansell* v *Abbey Life Assurance Co Ltd* supra is a decision which exemplifies this approach to construction.

It follows in practical terms that employers or businesses will find that they owe duties to workers who are not their own directly employed employees and accordingly will need to take steps to accommodate those workers. Failure to do so might result in a liability being incurred where the existence of a duty is not appreciated until after it has been breached. It follows that lawyers advising in these cases might find additional or alternative respondents beyond the nominal employer and that disabled people have more protection under the law than might appear to be the case.

The extension of discrimination provisions to trade organisations is a logical step. Membership of a trade union, a body such as the Law Society or the Bar Council, might be a significant part of someone's working life and it would be anomalous if a disabled person has protection from an enlightened employer but no protection from an unscrupulous or discriminatory trade organisation. The dual structure of discrimination taking place by way of less favourable treatment or a breach of what is termed a section 15 duty to take reasonable steps, mirrors the structure which applies to employment relationships, with certain modifications.

Advertisements are the subject of a special provision in the DDA 1995, and interestingly, raise a presumption of discrimination should the five criteria specified in the DDA 1995 be met. This is distinct from the position when a recipient fails to respond to a questionnaire. Many job adverts will be fairly bland and uninformative, with discrimination taking place at selection for interview or interview. It remains to be seen how significant the anti-discrimination provisions in relation to adverts will be, but the impact is unlikely to be significant. The presumption will be rebutted in any event, if the advertiser introduces evidence which counters the presumption of discrimination.

The provisions in relation to leasehold premises, are clearly of great significance. They modify third party rights and interfere with the freedom of contract, insofar as implied terms are created into a lease. But they remove any excuse based on a lease that an employer or other might have for refusing to alter premises and raise the possibility that a landlord who knows nothing of the disabled person's circumstances will find himself joined into a discrimination claim.

The provisions dealing with occupational pensions and insurance services will be of little significance for most employment claims which will hinge upon questions relating to such matters as dismissal and working practices.

SUMMARY

- The purposive interpretation of the DDA 1995 received a fillip in the decision of the Court of Appeal in *Tansell* v *Abbey Life Assurance Co Ltd* which gives a wide protection to contract workers within the ambit of the DDA 1995.
- Trade organisations such as trade unions, professional bodies are also caught by provisions of the DDA 1995, in recognition of the substantial role many such bodies have in working life.
- Specific provision is made in respect of advertisements which might be discriminatory in nature but the provisions are likely to be of limited significance.
- Third party and landlord rights are altered by the implication of terms into leasehold agreements.
- The ambit of protection from discrimination in the employment context extends into the provision of occupational pension schemes and insurance services.

CHAPTER SEVEN
PROCEDURE IN THE EMPLOYMENT TRIBUNAL

SYNOPSIS

The employment tribunal functions on an informal basis and without a great degree of procedural complexity. Procedural rules do exist and these can be used to further a case. This chapter examines the source of such rules, their scope and potential employment.

THE CONCEPTS

The first point that consideration of the current procedural rules raises, is that they have been rewritten as a result of a review of tribunal procedure. The rules are now to be found in the Employment Tribunals (Constitution and Rules of Procedure) Regulations 2001. These rules came into force on 18 April 2001. The rules are grounded in concepts contained in the Civil Procedure Rules.

THE EMPLOYMENT TRIBUNALS (CONSTITUTION AND RULES OF PROCEDURE) REGULATIONS 2001

These regulations are essentially a restatement of the Employment Tribunals (Constitution and Rules of Procedure) Regulations 1993 and provide for the establishment of employment tribunals, the appointment of their members, regional chairmen and most significantly rules of procedure governing the conduct of complaints. These rules are contained in Schedule 1 to the regulations. Certain of the regulations are worthy of note, including regulation 10, which provides that:

(1) The overriding objective of the rules in Schedules 1, 2, 3, 4, 5 and 6 is to enable tribunals to deal with cases justly.

(2) Dealing with a case justly includes, so far as is practicable –
  (a) ensuring that the parties are on an equal footing;
  (b) saving expense;
  (c) dealing with the case in ways which are proportionate to the complexity of the issues; and
  (d) ensuring that it is dealt with expeditiously and fairly.

(3) A tribunal shall seek to give effect to the overriding objective when it –
  (a) exercises any power given to it by the rules in schedules 1, 2, 3, 4, 5 and 6; or
  (b) interprets any rules in Schedules 1, 2, 3, 4, 5 and 6.

(4) The parties shall assist the tribunal to further the overriding objective.

SCHEDULE 1 THE EMPLOYMENT TRIBUNALS RULES OF PROCEDURE

The rules contain the following significant provisions that are summarised by way of table:

Rule 1	this provides that proceedings brought in the tribunal are to be by way of originating application and accordingly set out a number of required elements that the originating application should contain.
Rule 2	provides for the receipt of the originating application and provides for its entry into the Register.
Rule 3	deals with the entry of an appearance to the originating application by the respondent to it, for the purposes of disability discrimination claims, the alleged discriminator. Time can be extended for entering an appearance.
Rule 4	gives the tribunal some interlocutory teeth, by allowing orders to be made for the provision of particulars and the giving of disclosure and inspection. Written answers to specific questions can be sought, and witnesses can be ordered to attend. The tribunal can also control its own procedure by providing that for non-compliance with such interlocutory orders an originating application or notice of appearance should be struck out.

Rule 5	deals with the fixing of a hearing.
Rule 6	deals with the ability of the tribunal to determine at a preliminary hearing whether a party is entitled to bring proceedings. In the context of the DDA 1995, this will normally involve an initial determination of whether the complainant is disabled within the definition of the Act.
Rule 7	is concerned with pre-hearing reviews. These are rarely ordered, but can take place and a tribunal will determine whether the application has a reasonable prospect of success. If the tribunal decides it does not have this prospect, the application is not dismissed, but the applicant has to pay a deposit of up to £500 and is at risk of an order of costs, should the application be lost on its hearing.
Rule 8	deals with the national security issues.
Rule 9	deals with dismissals in connection with industrial action.
Rule 10	deals with the hearing.
Rule 11	governs the conduct of the hearing, and makes plain that formal rules of evidence do not apply. It also provides for evidence to be given on oath.
Rule 12	deals with the decision of the tribunal.
Rule 13	allows a review of a tribunal's decision in limited circumstances.
Rule 14	is concerned with costs which can be made when a party or a party's representative has acted vexatiously, abusively, disruptively, or otherwise unreasonably of the bringing or conducting of the proceedings has been misconceived.
Rule 15	deals with miscellaneous powers.
Rule 16	gives the tribunal a power to make a restricted reporting order.
Rule 17	is concerned with extensions of time.

Rule 18	is concerned with devolution issues.
Rule 19	is concerned with joinder of parties
Rule 20	is concerned with the combination of proceedings.
Rule 21	deals with the transfer of proceedings between England and Wales and Scotland.
Rule 22	allows references to the European Court of Justice.
Rule 23	makes provision for notices and documents.

STRATEGIC CONSIDERATIONS

The employment tribunal lends itself to informality, a quasi-inquisitorial approach and a focus on the issues rather than the letter of procedural rules. But the tribunal rules are of considerable significance and, used properly, can greatly assist in the presentation of a complaint or in its defence.

The formal rules of pleading or statements of case do not apply in the tribunal. This has led to vague or handwritten originating applications being put in that raise serious allegations of discrimination which are wholly unparticularised. It follows that in every case, a respondent should give consideration to a request for further particulars or for written answers to questions, so that the respondent knows the case it has to meet at the hearing and, if the applicant departs from that case, legitimate comment can be made on his credibility. Conversely an applicant is also entitled to seek particulars of an assertion that, for example, failure to comply with a section 6 duty is justified. In substantial cases, disclosure might be sought, in order for relevant documents to be produced, probably by the respondent.

The utility of these rules is not confined to the initial hearing on liability. As noted in the case of *Buxton* v *Equinox Design Ltd*, disability discrimination cases can involve substantial claims for compensation and it is appropriate for a further raft of directions to be given in respect of any remedies hearing, so that for example, schedules of loss, disclosure of an applicant's wage details, job applications and similar documentation which evidences attempts to mitigate loss are provided well in advance of a hearing.

Of the various types of preliminary hearing, many tribunals will make orders for the hearing of whether an applicant is disabled within the meaning of the DDA 1995 as a preliminary issue. This can generate significant extra costs and its utility must be questioned, where for example there is a claim for unfair dismissal which will continue irrespective of the decision on the disability discrimination point. Conversely for respondents, such a preliminary hearing often represents a chance to knock out a discrimination claim at a relatively early stage.

A major gap in the armoury of tribunal's interlocutory armoury is the absence of an ability to give summary judgment or otherwise deal with a weak claim except by requiring a deposit.

Costs are infrequently awarded in the tribunal. Nonetheless steps can be taken to lay a paper trail of correspondence to present to the tribunal, of steps taken which it is contended, represent unreasonable conduct on the part of the other side. Similarly old style *Calderbank* letters can be written, "without prejudice save as to costs". These are likely to be of limited utility before most tribunals, but the guiding principle when applying for costs, is that it never hurts to ask!

SUMMARY

- The current procedural rules which apply in employment tribunals are to be found in schedule 1 to the Employment Tribunals (Constitution and Rules of Procedure) Regulations 2001.
- The current procedural rules are the result of a revision of tribunal procedure.
- Changes in the rules from the old 1993 rules, reflect the Civil Procedure Rules applied in the civil courts.
- The prudent lawyer will ensure that the interlocutory stages of a disability discrimination case are carefully conducted so that the maximum possible advantage is extracted from the rules.
- In many disability discrimination cases, where the issue of disability is contentious the tribunal will order a preliminary hearing which will determine whether the applicant is entitled to bring the proceedings.

CHAPTER EIGHT
REMEDIES IN THE EMPLOYMENT TRIBUNAL

SYNOPSIS

The practice in employment tribunals is to determine the issue of liability before that of remedy. Indeed after a hard fought hearing on liability, the issue of remedy will often be adjourned. In the interim before the reconvened hearing, the parties may be able to settle the case. If this does not occur, the tribunal will consider what remedy should be given to the successful applicant.

THE CONCEPTS

The majority of applicants to a tribunal will simply be interested in an award of compensation. But this is not the limit of the tribunal's powers: it does have the option to grant other remedies, though it is to be anticipated that the majority of awards will consist purely of compensation.

The approach that should be adopted in remedies hearings in the employment tribunal was established in the employment appeal tribunal's decision in the case of *Buxton* v *Equinox Design Ltd* [1999] IRLR 158. In this case the EAT held:

- tribunals must be alert to problems that may arise in remedy hearings in disability discrimination cases;
- where a case involved unlimited compensation, often careful preparation and judicial management will be appropriate;
- directions may be made for the exchange of statements of case and witness statements;

- in some disability cases, a medical expert may be required and special consideration should be given to fixing the hearing to accommodate a busy professional witness.

THE EMPLOYMENT TRIBUNAL'S POWERS

When an employment tribunal rules that a complaint of discrimination is established it has the power to utilise a number of potential remedies, per section 8(2) DDA 1995:

> (2) Where an employment tribunal finds that a complaint presented to it under this section is well-founded, it shall take such of the following steps as it considers just and equitable –
> (a) making a declaration as to the rights of the complainant and the respondent in relation to the matters to which the complaint relates;
> (b) ordering the respondent to pay compensation to the complainant;
> (c) recommending that the respondent take, within a specified period, action appearing to the tribunal to be reasonable in all the circumstances of the case, for the purpose of obviating or reducing the adverse effect on the complainant of any matter to which the complaint relates.

Each of these remedies will be considered in turn below.

A DECLARATION

What is a declaration? At its simplest, it will be a statement that the successful complainant has been discriminated against. This may be of some moral comfort to an individual complainant but will be of scant financial significance to him. The chief value of a declaration might well be geared at altering practices in the workplace thereby affording tangible relief to the individual applicant, as the declaration must be framed in terms of the particular dispute between the applicant and the respondent. Broad sweeping statements would fall out with the ambit of the DDA 1995, narrow statements focussing on a particular individual and his complaint can be the subject of a declaration.

A RECOMMENDATION

Recommendations will be made by a tribunal where a particular working relationship continues. They will have no utility where the complainant has no continuing relationship with the respondent. They must also be framed in general terms, perhaps requiring a respondent to consider steps to take to comply with a section 6 duty. Specific steps, such as ordering an employer to allow an epileptic to operate potentially dangerous machinery might put the employer in breach of health and safety provisions, and would not be appropriate or indeed lawful.

Recommendations which are not complied with carry an adverse penalty:

> (5) If the respondent fails, without reasonable justification, to comply with a recommendation made by an employment tribunal under subsection (2)(c) the tribunal may, if it thinks it just and equitable to do so –
> (a) increase the amount of compensation required to be paid to the complainant in respect of the complaint, where an order was made under subsection (2)(b); or
> (b) make an order under subsection (2)(b).

COMPENSATION

Undoubtedly the most frequently resorted to remedy under the DDA 1995 will be an award of compensation. An award of compensation under this statute, as in cases of sexual and racial discrimination, is unlimited.

The DDA 1995 specifies the basis on which compensation is to be awarded:

> (3) Where a tribunal orders compensation under subsection (2)(b), the amount of the compensation shall be calculated by applying the principles applicable to the calculation of damages in claims in tort or (in Scotland) in reparation for breach of statutory duty.
>
> (4) For the avoidance of doubt, it is hereby declared that compensation in respect of discrimination in a way which is unlawful under this Part may include compensation under any other head.

Thus the measure of damages differs from that under the Employment Rights Act 1996 with its use of the principle of "just and equitable" compensation. The measure of damages under the DDA 1995 is tortious and that means that the complainant is entitled to be put back into the position he would have been in had the tort not occurred. Subsection (3) however, makes it plain there is to be an additional head of damage, not usually recognised in tort, that of compensation for injury to feelings, resulting from the discrimination. The likely measure of such damages can be obtained by considering the *Judicial Studies Board Guidelines (5th edition)* which deal with quantum of damages for pain and suffering for psychiatric harm. In addition, for a measure of damages see *Employment Law & Litigation* (EMIS Professional Publishing).

THE SETTLEMENT OF A COMPLAINT

In affiliation with other employment and discrimination related provisions, the DDA 1995 is concerned to prevent employees from "contracting out", or being made to "contract out" of the anti-discrimination provisions. Terms which purport to limit or exclude the application of the DDA 1995 or which require persons to do anything which would contravene the DDA 1995 or which prevent them from making complaints to the employment tribunal are void (section 9(1) DDA 1995).

No absolute bar is made on settling a claim made under the DDA 1995, but procedural safeguards are put in place to protect the rights of applicants when settling cases. Thus the services of ACAS or a qualified lawyer must be used if a settlement of proceedings is to be obtained.

Section 9(2) provides:

> (2) Paragraphs (b) and (c) of subsection (1) do not apply to an agreement not to institute proceedings under section 8(1), or to an agreement not to continue such proceedings, if –
> (a) a conciliation officer has acted under paragraph 1 of Schedule 3 in relation to the matter; or
> (b) the conditions set out in subsection (3) are satisfied.

The conditions are that –

- the complainant must have received independent legal advice from a qualified lawyer as to the terms and effect of the proposed agreement (and in particular its effect on his ability to pursue his complaint before an employment tribunal);
- when the adviser gave the advice there must have been in force a policy of insurance covering the risk of a claim by the complainant in respect of loss arising in consequence of the advice; and

- the agreement must be in writing, relate to the particular complaint, identify the adviser and state that the conditions are satisfied.

STRATEGIC CONSIDERATIONS

The provisions of the DDA 1995 which deal with remedies are non-controversial. It is doubtful whether declarations or recommendations will prove to be of much significance in the majority of cases, where the complainant's concerns will be to obtain as large an award of compensation as possible. Where declarations or recommendations will prove to be of significance is when a number of claims are brought arising out of common working practices. Similarly claims for disability discrimination will undoubtedly be brought, where dismissal of the disabled complainant has not occurred. The complainant might simply be seeking a recommendation that his working practices be changed and a relatively modest amount of compensation for his injury to feelings. In that instance, considerable thought must be devoted to the wording of any declaration or recommendation that the tribunal is asked to make, to ensure it is a remedy that the tribunal has power to give and is not otherwise unlawful or requires the respondent to act, for example, in breach of health and safety legislation.

SUMMARY

- An employment tribunal can make a declaration, a recommendation or order compensation dependent on what it considers to be just and equitable.
- The principle remedy which applicants will seek is compensation.
- Compensation is to be assessed on the tortious basis and will include an award for injury to feelings.
- Declarations and recommendations must be lawful: framed within the terms of the DDA 1995 and not requiring a respondent to take steps that might conflict with other legal requirements.
- Additional compensation can be awarded to a complainant if a recommendation is made and not complied with.

CHAPTER NINE
THE JURISDICTION OF THE COUNTY COURT

SYNOPSIS

The preceding chapters have considered the jurisdiction of the employment tribunal, which is concerned with disability discrimination in the field of employment. The ambit of the DDA 1995 is wider than the employment sphere and includes discrimination in the provision of services. This chapter considers discrimination in the field of services, goods and facilities.

THE CONCEPTS

Discrimination against disabled people is not only outlawed in the context of the employment relationship, but also in terms of the provision of goods and services to that section of the general public who are disabled. Part III of the DDA 1995 is concerned to provide redress for discrimination cases outside the employment context. The forum for proceedings is not the employment tribunal, but in England and Wales the county court.

The principal provisions of Part III are concerned with the provision of services and housing.

THE JURISDICTION OF THE COUNTY COURT

Section 25 DDA 1995 gives the county court its jurisdiction:

> (1) A claim by a person that another person –
> (a) has discriminated against him in a way which is unlawful under this Part; or

(b) is by virtue of section 57 and 58 to be treated as having discriminated against him in such a way may be made the subject of civil proceedings in the same way as any other claim in tort...

(2) Proceedings in England and Wales shall be brought only in a county court.

Section 25 is supplemented by further provisions dealing with the bringing of a claim in Part II of Schedule 3 to the DDA 1995 (section 25(6)). The provisions are chiefly concerned with establishing time limits for the claims to be brought.

TIME LIMITS FOR BRINGING A CLAIM

Part II of Schedule 3 DDA 1995 (para 6) provides as follows:

(1) A county court or sheriff court shall not consider a claim under section 25 unless proceedings in respect of the claim are instituted before the end of the period of six months beginning when the act complained of was done.

(3) A court may consider any claim under section 25 which is out of time if, in all the circumstances of the case, it considers that it is just and equitable to do so.

(4) For the purposes of sub-paragraph (1) –
   (a) where an unlawful act of discrimination is attributable to a term in a contract, that act is to be treated as extending throughout the duration of the contract;
   (b) any act extending over a period shall be treated as done at the end of that period; and
   (c) a deliberate omission shall be treated as done when the person in question decided upon it.

(5) In the absence of evidence establishing the contrary, a person shall be taken for the purposes of this paragraph to decide upon an omission-
   (a) when he does an act inconsistent with doing the omitted act; or
   (b) if he has done no such inconsistent act, when the period expires within which he might reasonably have been expected to do the omitted act if it was to be done.

EXEMPTIONS FROM THE PROVISIONS OF PART III

The provisions of Part III do not apply to educational services, as defined by the DDA 1995 (Section 19(5)-(6)) nor do they apply to services so far as they consist of the use of any means of transport (19(5)(b)) or other services which might be prescribed (19(5)(c)). Further exemptions are given in relation to the provision of housing, if the housing in question falls within the scope of the exemption contained within section 23 DDA 1995. This is principally concerned with small premises as defined within that section.

THE AMBIT OF DISCRIMINATION

The opening section of Part III of the DDA 1995 provides:

> (1) It is unlawful for a provider of services to discriminate against a disabled person –
> (a) in refusing to provide, or deliberately not providing, to the disabled person any service which he provides or is prepared to provide, to members of the public;
> (b) in failing to comply with any duty imposed on him by section 21 in circumstances in which the effect of that failure is to make it impossible or unreasonably difficult for the disabled person to make use of any such service;
> (c) in the standard of the service which he provides to the disabled person or the manner in which he provides it to him; or
> (d) in the terms on which he provides a service to the disabled person.

A number of examples are provided (at section 19(3)) of services to which the anti-discrimination provisions would apply:

- Access to and use of any place which members of the public are permitted to enter.
- Access to and use of means of communication.
- Access to and use of information services.
- Accommodation in a hotel, boarding house or other similar establishment.
- Facilities by way of banking, or insurance or for grants loans, credit or finance.

- Facilities for entertainment, recreation, or refreshment.
- Facilities provided by employment agencies or under section 2 of the Employment and Training Act 1973
- The services of any profession or trade, or any local or other public authority.

THE MEANING OF DISCRIMINATION

A similar approach, although with a number of key differences, is adopted to the definition of discrimination within the context of a Part III claim as exists in a Part II claim. The DDA 1995 provides at section 20:

(1) For the purposes of section 19, a provider of services discriminates against a disabled person if –
  (a) for a reason which relates to the disabled person's disability, he treats him less favourably than he treats or would treat others to whom that reason does not or would not apply; and
  (b) he cannot show that the treatment in question is justified.

(2) For the purposes of section 19 a provider of services also discriminates against a disabled person if –
  (a) he fails to comply with a section 21 duty imposed on him in relation to the disabled person; and
  (b) he cannot show that his failure to comply with that duty is justified.

STRATEGIC CONSIDERATIONS

Part III of the DDA 1995 has only had a very limited impact in terms of litigation. This could be because there is little or no discrimination against the disabled by the providers of services but more likely is due to the inherent limitations in a county court action for the statutory tort of disability discrimination.

This is because the statutory tort of discrimination will normally be worth very little in terms of quantum, being limited to a claim for damages for injuries to feelings. In the normal course of events such a claim falls to be allocated to the Small Claims track, where a no costs rule will effectively render pointless or prohibitive in expense any litigation conducted by lawyers. Few people, disabled or not, would wish to take on the role of litigant in person.

The time limits which apply to civil proceedings are not greatly in excess of the limits which apply to tribunal proceedings. Six months is the operative limit with the provision that the period can be extended where it is just and equitable to do so.

There is no authority as to how this judicial discretion to disapply the limitation period is to be exercised. Most judges will have experience of section 33 of the Limitation Act 1980 and perhaps a similar approach will be adopted to considering applications to disapply the limitation period which applies to personal injury cases under that section.

Exemptions also exist under this part of the Act, with the fields of education and transport specifically excluded from the ambit of the Act. There are limitations in relation to the provision of housing, but these are principally concerned to protect the rights of occupiers. It is not immediately apparent that these exemptions would give rise to incompatibility with the provisions of the European Convention on Human Rights, particularly as they involve questions of resources and also the rights of individuals in relation to their homes.

Section 21 duties differ materially from their counterpart section 6 and section 15 duties found in Part II of the DDA 1995, a difference which will be explored further in this work.

The emphasis in Part III of the DDA 1995 is to deal with failures to provide services, failings in the standard of service or the terms on which services are provided as well as a failure to comply with section 21 duties.

SUMMARY

- Part III of the DDA 1995 establishes the county court in England and Wales as the forum for actions for the statutory tort of disability discrimination in the field of services.
- Part III has generated a tiny amount of litigation, and could be regarded as a failure or success in this respect, depending on one's perspective.

- The time limit on bringing proceedings can be extended on a just and equitable basis. It remains to be seen what approach the courts will take to this test.
- Significant areas, such as transport and the provision of education are exempted from the provisions of the DDA 1995.
- The limitations inherent in proceedings on the Small Claims track are likely render pointless any actions for discrimination in the county court on the conventional basis.

CHAPTER TEN

LESS FAVOURABLE TREATMENT BY SERVICE PROVIDERS

SYNOPSIS

Less favourable treatment together with a failure to comply with section 21 duties, are the twin forms of discrimination prohibited by Part III of the DDA 1995. This chapter considers the concept of less favourable treatment in the provision of services.

THE CONCEPTS

Less favourable treatment or direct discrimination as it is often called, as noted in the preceding chapters of this work, is theoretically a straightforward concept.

THE CONCEPT OF LESS FAVOURABLE TREATMENT

The wording of section 20(1) reads:

> (1) For the purposes of this Part, a provider of services discriminates against a disabled person if –
> (a) for a reason which relates to the disabled person's disability he treats him less favourably than he treats or would treat others to whom that reason does not or would not apply; and
> (b) he cannot show that the treatment in question is justified.

The section requires a number of distinct elements to be proved for discrimination to be established. There must be:

- a causal link between treatment and a reason related to a disabled person's disability;
- less favourable treatment compared to others to whom the disability related reason does not apply;
- no justification for the less favourable treatment.

If these three elements are met, then a finding of discrimination can be made.

THE REASON FOR THE TREATMENT MUST BE RELATED TO THE DISABILITY

The wording of section 20(1), with the requirement that less favourable treatment must be related to the disability requires a causal link to be established between a disabled person's disability and what may appear to be unjustified less favourable treatment. It is open to a court to find less favourable treatment but that this was for a non-disability related reason.

A further point which arises from this requirement, is whether a service provider who claims to be ignorant of a disabled person's disability, can therefore establish that such ignorance precludes any less favourable treatment being for a reason related to a disability, as the service provider lacked the necessary knowledge to discriminate. In the employment context this question has resulted in a division of opinion in the employment appeal tribunal. No decision has been reported in the civil courts as to whether knowledge is a necessary requirement.

The sole case which deals with whether "the reason for the treatment is related to the disability" is *R* v *Powys CC Ex p Hambidge* [2000] 54 BMLR 133. This case does not sit easily with the approach adopted by Mummery LJ in the case of *Clark* v *TDG Ltd t/a Novacold* supra.

THE OTHERS TO WHOM THAT REASON DOES NOT OR WOULD NOT APPLY

The requirement that less favourable treatment is to be assessed against the treatment afforded to other persons, to whom disability related reasons do not apply imports ostensibly into disability discrimination law the concept of a comparator, a concept easily recognisable in other branches of discrimination law.

The potential problem that this created, already noted in the employment context, is who the comparator was to be? Was it a simply a person without a disability or a person with the same characteristics as a disabled person without a disability? The problem was firmly grasped by the Court of Appeal in the case of *Clark* v *TDG Ltd t/a Novacold* and the reasoning of that decision should apply to cases under Part III of the DDA 1995.

THE PROVISIONS OF THE CODE OF PRACTICE

The *Code of Practice* also gives some guidance (paras 3.4-3.7). Paragraph 3.4 reads:

> For a disabled person to be discriminated against in this way, he or she must have been treated less favourably by a service provide in comparison with how the service provider treats (or would treat) other people....
>
> The disability-related treatment of the disabled person is compared with how the service provider treats (or would treat) other people to whom the disability-related reason does not apply.

In simple terms the comparator is not a person in like for like circumstances; the focus is on the reason for the treatment, as compared to the way others are or would be treated. Thus as the *Code* makes clear (para 3.9) disabled people using sign language who are refused admission to a disco, on the basis that the doorman would refuse entry to anyone making "strange" gestures, will still constitute discrimination.

JUSTIFICATION

A key difference between Part II claims and Part III claims is the definition of the defence of justification. Justification can only be established if the following criteria are reached:

> (3) For the purposes of this section, treatment is justified only if:
> (a) in the opinion of the provider of services, one or more of the conditions mentioned in subsection (4) are satisfied; and
> (b) it is reasonable, in all the circumstances of the case, for him to hold that opinion.

The particular conditions which are specified in subsection (4) that mean justification might be possible are:

- In any case the treatment is necessary in order not to endanger the health or safety of any person (which may include that of the disabled person).
- In any case the disabled person is incapable of entering into an enforceable agreement, or of giving an informed consent and for that reason the treatment is reasonable in that case.
- In a case falling within section 19(1)(a) the treatment is necessary because the provider of services would otherwise be unable to provide the service to members of the public.
- In a case falling within section 19(1)(c) or (d), the treatment is necessary in order for the provider of services to be able to provide the service to the disabled person or other members of the public.
- In a case falling within section 19(1)(d) the difference in the terms on which the service is provided to the disabled person and those on which it is provided to other members of the public reflects the greater cost to the provider of services in providing the service to the disabled person.

Regard should also be had to a further criteria:

> (5) Any increase in the cost of providing a service to a disabled person which results from compliance by a provider of services with a section 21 duty shall be disregarded for the purposes of subsection 4(e).

Regard should also be had to the Disability Discrimination (Services and Premises) Regulations 1996, SI 1996/1836 which deal with particular instances of when less favourable treatment is justified.

STRATEGIC CONSIDERATIONS

The *Code of Practice on Rights of Access, Goods, Facilities, Services and Premises* is of crucial importance in considering Part III claims due to the paucity of authority on the interpretation and application of the provisions. Nonetheless the application of the provisions should prove to be relatively straightforward.

The discrimination provisions are concerned to provide a disabled person with a remedy when a service provider refuses to provide or deliberately does not provide services which would otherwise be offered to the public, provides services which are of a lower standard or in a worse manner or provides services on worse terms.

In terms of the refusal to provide services, the *Code of Practice* makes it plain (paras 3.12-3.14) that a refusal to serve a disabled person will be unlawful and that the motive for doing so is irrelevant. Thus if a service provider genuinely believes he cannot cater for a disabled person or that a better service could be provided somewhere else, this is no defence under the DDA 1995.

Lower standards of service can include harassment, being offhand to disabled people, or simple rudeness (para 3.15). The *Code of Practice* also makes the point (para 3.16) that, for example, although a service provider does not have to stock special products for disabled people, if the service provider would normally take orders from non-disabled customers for special products, a failure to order such items as large print books is likely to be discriminatory.

Worse terms include charging more for goods, without justification or imposing extra conditions for using a service. The *Code of Practice* gives the example (at para 3.17) of a partially sighted disabled applicant for a loan, who is told by the lender that due to his disability, his signature must be witnessed by a solicitor.

The focus in Part III cases of less favourable treatment is very much on the reason for the treatment given and whether it is attributable to a disability related reason. Problems with comparators should not arise, in part due to the Court of Appeal decision in *Clark* v *TDG Ltd t/a Novacold* supra but also due to the fact that most county court judges will approach the DDA 1995 afresh, without preconceptions derived from experience of sex and race discrimination claims.

A very significant point to note in relation to the defence of justification, is the difference between the defence in the employment context and the provision of services. The service provider who wishes to establish the defence of justification must now establish a reason which is one of the five specified within the Act. Failure to do so, will preclude the defence of justification being raised. The reason must be established on the evidence. The subjective belief of the service provider that the reason is established, will then be tested by the application of an objective criterion of reasonableness, to ensure that obtuse or bigoted service providers cannot rely on their own subjective opinions as a defence to a discrimination claim.

SUMMARY

- Less favourable treatment is the same concept within Part III as within Part II but differs in its application to the provision of services.
- The *Code of Practice* in the absence of appellate authority is of crucial importance in interpreting the provisions.
- Although no appellate authority has considered the issue of the comparator in practical terms this should not prove to be a difficulty.
- The defence of justification can be raised in relation to these claims but is materially different to the defence of justification in employment claims.
- Justification requires a service provider to have a subjective belief that one of five reasons justifies the treatment but this is qualified by the objective criterion of reasonableness.

CHAPTER ELEVEN

REASONABLE ADJUSTMENTS BY SERVICE PROVIDERS

SYNOPSIS

Less favourable treatment is only the first limb of a potential discrimination claim, as the failure to take reasonable steps to comply with a section 21 duty also constitutes discrimination. There are similarities with section 6 and section 15 duties, but also important differences. This chapter considers how section 21 works in practice.

THE CONCEPTS

The section 21 duties, to make reasonable adjustments differ from the section 6 duties imposed upon an employer.

THE SECTION 21 DUTIES

Section 21(1) provides:

> (1) Where a provider of services has a practice, policy or procedure which makes it impossible or unreasonably difficult for disabled persons to make use of a service which he provides, or is prepared to provide, to other members of the public, it is his duty to take such steps as it is reasonable, in all the circumstances of the case, for him to have to take in order to change that practice, policy or procedure so that it no longer has that effect.
>
> (2) Where a physical feature (for example, one arising from the design or construction of a building or the approach or access to the premises) makes it impossible or unreasonably difficult for disabled persons to make use of such a service, it is the duty of the

provider of that service to take such steps as it is reasonable, in all the circumstances for him to have to take in order to

(a) remove the feature;
(b) alter it so that it no longer has that effect;
(c) provide a reasonable means of avoiding the feature; or
(d) provide a reasonable alternative method of making the service in question available to disabled persons.

It should be noted that of these four potential steps prescribed by the section, only the step required by part (d) is currently in force. It is anticipated that section 21(2)(a) to (c) will be brought into force in 2004.

Subsection (4) also provides:

(4) Where an auxiliary aid or service (for example the provision of information on audio tape or of a sign language interpreter) would –

(a) enable disabled persons to make use of a service which a provider of services provides, or is prepared to provide, to members of the public, or
(b) facilitate the use by disabled persons of such a service, it is the duty of the provider of that service to take such steps as it is reasonable , in all the circumstances of the case, for him to have to take in order to provide that auxiliary aid or service.

POTENTIAL REASONABLE STEPS TO TAKE

The section 21 duties differ from the section 6 duties in that there is no corresponding subsection to subsection 6(3), which gives examples of steps to be taken in compliance with the duties. Rather, reference has to be made to the Code of Practice by service providers in order to put flesh onto the bones of the duties established by the Act. The Code currently in force is not the original version, but rather a new and updated version which was brought into force by the Disability Discrimination (Services and Premises) Regulations 1999 SI 1999/1191 on 1st October 1999, in order to provide additional guidance on the steps which need to be taken in relation to physical features.

WHEN IT WILL BE REASONABLE TO TAKE STEPS

Section 6(4), which in relation to employment provisions provides criteria for determining when it is reasonable for an employer to have to take a particular step has no parallel in the Part III provisions. Instead section 21(5), is an enabling section which allows regulations to be made providing for (amongst other things) what circumstances will or will not make it reasonable for a service provider to take particular steps.

THE REQUIREMENT OF KNOWLEDGE

A further difference between the section 6 and section 21 duties, is that no requirement of knowledge is prescribed by section 21. The service provider does not have to know that a particular person is disabled or that there is a need for a particular step to be taken. Section 21, provides duties which have to be complied with in relation to the world in general, including that proportion of the public which is disabled, so there is no requirement of knowledge which would be otiose and probably render the duties unenforceable.

EXCLUSIONS FROM THE DUTY TO TAKE REASONABLE STEPS

It has already been noted above, that parts of section 21, which deal with alterations to physical features are not in force.

It should also be noted that there are two general exclusions in the body of the section:

> (6) Nothing in this section requires a provider of services to take any steps that would fundamentally alter the nature of the service in question or the nature of his trade, profession or business.
>
> (7) Nothing in this section requires a provider of services to take any steps that would cause him to incur expenditure exceeding the prescribed maximum.

THE DEFENCE OF JUSTIFICATION

The defence of justification is also available in respect of a failure to comply with a section 21 duty. Section 20(9) provides that the same considerations that apply to justification in less favourable treatment cases, also apply in relation to cases that are concerned with the failure to comply with a section 21 duties.

> (3) For the purposes of this section, treatment is justified only if –
>
> (a) in the opinion of the provider of services, one or more of the conditions mentioned in subsection (4) are satisfied; and

(b) it is reasonable, in all the circumstances of the case, for him to hold that opinion.

The particular conditions which are specified in subsection (4) that mean that justification might be possible are:

- In any case the treatment is necessary in order not to endanger the health or safety of any person (which may include that of the disabled person).
- In any case the disabled person is incapable of entering into an enforceable agreement, or of giving an informed consent and for that reason the treatment is reasonable in that case.
- In a case falling within section 19(1)(a) the treatment is necessary because the provider of services would otherwise be unable to provide the service to members of the public.
- In a case falling within section 19(1)(c) or (d), the treatment is necessary in order for the provider of services to be able to provide the service to the disabled person or other members of the public.
- In a case falling within section 19(1)(d) the difference in the terms on which the service is provided to the disabled person and those on which it is provided to other members of the public reflects the greater cost to the provider of services in providing the service to the disabled person.

Regard should also be had to a further criterion:

(4) Any increase in the cost of providing a service to a disabled person which results from compliance by a provider of services with a section 21 duty shall be disregarded for the purposes of subsection 4(e).

STRATEGIC CONSIDERATIONS

Section 21 requires service providers to alter their practices, policies or procedures which make it impossible or unreasonably difficult for disabled persons to make use of their services. Section 21 also imposes a duty where a physical feature of the service provider's building makes it impossible or unreasonably difficult, for a disabled person to make use of the service for steps to be taken to remove that impossibility or difficulty. It should be noted that this latter aspect of the section 21 duty, is seen as controversial and the section is not fully in force, in order to afford to service providers a number of years in order to take steps so they are "section 21 compliant". The only duty that is currently in force is the duty to provide a reasonable alternative method of making services available, rather than the duties that require a service provider to take action to alter or remove a physical feature of the premises or to provide a reasonable means of avoiding the physical feature.

Practices, policies and procedures according to the *Code of Practice* include what a service provider does, what it intends to do and how it plans to go about it (para 5.4).

The obligation to take steps to remove the impossibility or difficulty is qualified by the criterion of reasonableness. However it is clear from the *Code of Practice* that the adequacy of the steps taken must be viewed purposively; tokenism that does not achieve desired results will not be viewed as reasonable.

Because the nature of the duties is a continuing one, steps taken initially that might seem reasonable might prove to be inadequate in practice. These steps would then have to be reviewed and perhaps additional steps taken. The *Code of Practice* gives the example of an out of town shopping centre, which makes specific car parking spaces next to the entrance available for the use of disabled persons only.

If these spaces are continually used by the public and so not in practice available to the disabled, then further steps such as car park patrols might need to be undertaken, in order to ensure that the spaces are in fact used by disabled people (*Code* para 5.7)

It is interesting to note that no requirement of knowledge is contained within section 21. This undoubtedly reflects the reality of the different relationships of employer/employee and service provider/customer. A requirement of knowledge in the context of what are likely to prove infrequent or even one-off transactions would render any duties redundant, as in very few circumstances will a service provider have knowledge of the needs, or even the existence of his disabled customer. Instead the focus of section 21 is on generalised duties to the public at large, or at least that proportion of it which is disabled.

The corollary to this generalised approach is that it requires more than a degree of pro-activism on the part of service providers. Otherwise the first that a service provider will know about the discriminatory effect of its policies, practices, procedures or premises, is when the letter before action arrives. It follows that the defence of justification will undoubtedly assume even greater importance in the context of section 21 duties, than in relation to claims for less favourable treatment.

Few service providers will make adequate provision for auxiliary aids or services. These will include the provision of special equipment or extra assistance to disabled people by specially trained staff. Auxiliary aids must be carefully chosen and also available and in working order.

A point that should be noted is that aids or services are not limited to aids to communication but can include the use of portable ramps for wheelchairs or cushions. It should be noted that there is a dividing line between such physical aids and the installation of devices, structures or equipment which necessitate making a permanent alteration to the physical fabric of the premises and which accordingly fall out with the provisions of this sub-section.

Once again in the absence of appellate authority, the *Code of Practice* receives an even greater significance than it might otherwise possess, as it will form the chief aid to the interpretation and application of the various provisions of Part III of the DDA 1995.

Finally the balance of the duties in relation to the physical features of service providers premises are expected to come into force in 2004. Few service providers will be aware of this provision and it might be that the requirement to carry out alterations will spark a greater awareness of disability discrimination issues, or alternatively a welter of claims.

SUMMARY

- Section 21 duties differ in material ways from section 6 and section 15 duties.
- The differences in the scope and nature of the duties reflect the differing relationships between an employer and employee and a service provider and a customer.
- The duties are not fully in force in relation to the alteration of the premises of a service provider.
- The provision of auxiliary aids is a freestanding duty and the aids, which must reasonably be provided, are not limited to aids to communication.

- The *Code of Practice* is of immense practical significance both because of the absence of appellate authority and also in enabling service providers to undertake a pro-active approach to their duties under the DDA 1995.

CHAPTER TWELVE
HOUSING PROVISION

SYNOPSIS

A further area in which disability discrimination litigation can occur is in housing provision. These claims will also fall within the ambit of Part III of the DDA 1995 and accordingly will be brought in the county court. This chapter looks briefly at the provisions.

THE CONCEPTS

Part III of the DDA 1995 also makes provision in relation to housing. The intention is to provide redress to disabled person who suffers discrimination in the provision of accommodation. The scope of the Part III provisions is sufficiently wide enough to place duties on persons who have the power to dispose of premises or who are engaged in the management of premises.

THE AMBIT OF DISCRIMINATION

Part III of the DDA 1995 sets out the ambit of unlawful discrimination in relation to housing. The first provision at section 22(1) focuses on people who have the power to dispose of premises:

> (1) It is unlawful for a person with the power to dispose of any premises to discriminate against a disabled person –
> (a) in the terms on which he offers to dispose of those premises to the disabled person;

(b) by refusing to dispose of those premises to the disabled person;
(c) in his treatment of the disabled person in relation to any list of persons in need of premises of that description.

It should be noted that these provisions do not apply to someone who is an owner occupier, unless the services of an estate agent are utilised or an advertisement is published (section 22(2) DDA 1995).

Similarly it is unlawful for a manager of premises to discriminate against a disabled person:

(3) It is unlawful for a person managing any premises to discriminate against a disabled person occupying those premises –
(a) in the way he permits the disabled person to make use of any benefits or facilities;
(b) by refusing or deliberately omitting to permit the disabled person to make use of any benefits or facilities;
(c) by evicting the disabled person, or subjecting him to any other detriment.

It should also be noted that it is possible for a person whose consent is require to dispose of any premises, by withholding his consent to discriminate against a disabled person (section 22(4) DDA 1995).

THE DEFINITION OF DISCRIMINATION

There is no comparable raft of duties analogous to those imposed by section 6 and section 21 DDA 1995. The only way that discrimination can take place is by way of less favourable treatment. Section 24(1) reads:

(1) For the purposes of section 22, a person ("A") discriminates against a disabled person if –
(a) for a reason which relates to the disabled person's disability, he treats him less favourably than he treats or would treat others to whom that reason does or would not apply; and
(b) he cannot show that the treatment in question is justified.

THE DEFENCE OF JUSTIFICATION

The defence of justification is further defined in terms which differ again from justification in the employment context or the simple provision of goods and services:

(2) For the purposes of this section treatment is justified only if –
(a) in A's opinion, one or more of the conditions mentioned in subsection (3) are satisfied; and
(b) it is reasonable, in all the circumstances of the case, for him to hold that opinion.

The conditions specified in subsection (3) that mean justification may be possible are:

- In any case, the treatment is necessary in order not to endanger the health and safety of any person (which may include that of the disabled person).
- In any case, the disabled person is incapable of entering into an enforceable agreement, or of giving an informed consent, and for that reason the treatment is reasonable in that case.
- In a case falling within section 22(3)(a) the treatment is necessary in order for the disabled person or the occupiers of other premises forming part of the building to make use of the benefit or facility.
- In a case falling within section 22(3)(b) the treatment is necessary in order for the occupiers of other premises forming part of the building to make use of the benefit or facility.

STRATEGIC CONSIDERATIONS

The provisions on housing discrimination are straightforward. In essence they are directed at landlords or managing agents who treat the disabled less favourably in a number of ways. Refusing to let premises, or charging a higher rent will obviously be unlawful. But so will be the actions of a managing agent who refuses to place people with any forms of disability on their waiting lists, perhaps under the excuse that they have no properties suitable for disabled people or which are adapted for them.

The less favourable treatment might not constitute discrimination if it is justified. Justification can only be found when a limited number of reasons apply. These include reasons of health or safety, incapacity or when treatment is necessary in order for the disabled person or other occupiers to use a benefit or facility.

The *Code of Practice* provides helpful examples of when less favourable treatment will be justified. For example, a landlord who refuses to let an upper story flat to a disabled person who has mobility problems. If the disabled person is unable to negotiate the stairs or use the fire escape in an emergency, the landlord could refuse to let the premises on grounds of health and safety. Provided it is reasonable for the landlord to hold that opinion, the refusal to let will be justified (*Code of Practice paragraph 8.35).*

The DDA 1995 gives an exemption to small dwellings and accordingly the provisions of the Act and the *Code of Practice* must be consulted first, in order to determine whether any potential claim for discrimination is likely to prove misconceived, due to the exemption.

SUMMARY

- The provision of housing is an importance service and specific provision is made in Part III of the DDA 1995 to prevent discrimination in this area.
- The provisions apply not only to landlords and vendors but to managing agents and estate agents too.
- The only type of discrimination recognised in this area is direct discrimination.
- The *Code of Practice* contains many helpful examples of the provisions in practice.
- Exemption provisions apply in relation to small dwellings, which should be considered carefully.

CHAPTER THIRTEEN
PROCEDURE IN THE COUNTY COURT

SYNOPSIS

Claims brought under the provisions of Part III of the DDA 1995 will be brought in the county court in England and Wales. This chapter looks briefly at the key procedural issues, which will apply in such cases, by reference to the Civil Procedure Rules.

THE CONCEPTS

A claim of disability discrimination pursuant to Part III of the DDA 1995 is made in England and Wales by way of action in the county court: the High Court has no jurisdiction to entertain such a claim.

Accordingly the claim will be by way of Claim Form as provided for by Part 7 of the Civil Procedure Rules. It will fall to be served in accordance with those rules and assuming that the claim is defended, a Defence will be entered by the defendant. The claim will then fall to be allocated, to either the Small Claims Track, Fast Track or Multi-track. There also exists the possibility that if a number of claims are being brought, a Group Litigation Order will be made.

THE SUBJECT MATTER OF A CLAIM

Most claims against service providers will be limited to claims for injury to feelings. As such they will almost inevitably be worth less than £5000 and will fall to be allocated to the Small Claims Track. But some claims might include elements of special damages, such as the additional cost of making alternative arrangements and it is not inconceivable that a claim, particularly in the context of housing provision might be worth a great deal of money.

Conversely there might be, a large number of claims against a single service provider, arising from the treatment of a large number of disabled people who have encountered the same discriminatory treatment or practice. In those circumstances, each claim might be worth a modest amount, but the large number of claims would merit consolidation or a Group Litigation Order, indicating that allocation to the Multi-track is appropriate.

Assuming that the case is in fact allocated to the Small Claims Track the appropriate rules fall to be considered.

THE RULES ON THE SMALL CLAIMS TRACK

The relevant rules are contained within part 27 of the Civil Procedure Rules and are summarised in the table opposite.

STRATEGIC CONSIDERATIONS

The difficulty with proceedings in the civil courts is that in the majority of cases where a disabled person is given shoddy service or refused entry to premises, the sole item of loss caused will be injury to feelings. Awards for injury to feelings, will rarely consist of sums greater than £5000. Thus such proceedings will normally be allocated to the Small Claims track, on the basis of value alone.

This acts as a powerful disincentive to litigate for an individual disabled person. Many disabled people will be of limited means and unable to afford legal representation. Even if legal representation can be obtained, the disabled person will if successful not normally recover the legal costs sustained. If damages are recovered, almost inevitably any legal costs incurred will swallow up the award.

Arguments do exist that even in cases where quantum is likely to be fundamentally modest, such cases should be allocated to the Fast Track. One argument could be that the issues involved in any disability discrimination case are too complex for the scope of a Small Claims Track hearing. A further argument could be that the decision on allocation should take account of articles 6 and 10 of the European Convention on Human Rights and cases should be allocated to the Fast Track, so that the disabled person can utilise the services of a lawyer.

THE RULES ON THE SMALL CLAIMS TRACK

Rule 27.1	sets out the scope of part 27 of the Civil Procedure Rules.
Rule 27.2	disapplies part 18, part 31, part 32 (except part 32.1) part 33, part 35 (except rules 35.1, 35.3, 35.7 and 35.8), part 36 and part 39 (except rule 39.2).
Rule 27.3	provides that the court can grant any final remedy in a small claim that is available on the Fast Track or Multi-track.
Rule 27.4	provides for the court after allocation to give directions dealing with the prosecution and disposal of the claim.
Rule 27.5	provides that no expert evidence may be adduced without the permission of the court.
Rule 27.6	provides that a court may fix a preliminary hearing for the consideration of the claim.
Rule 27.7	makes it plain that the court can alter directions as it thinks fit.
Rule 27.8	gives an indication of how the hearing is to be conducted.
Rule 27.9	allows a claim to be determined in the absence of a party.
Rule 27.10	allows the court to dispose of a claim without a hearing if the parties agree.
Rule 27.11	allows a party to apply to set aside an award made in his absence.
Rules 27.12 and 27.13	which dealt with appeals have been revoked and appeals are now made under part 52 of the Civil Procedure Rules.
Rule 27.14	deals with costs and the very limited provisions which allow costs to be ordered in the Small Claims Court.
Rule 27.15	deals with costs after a claim is reallocated from the Small Claims track to another track.

The rules are also supplemented by a Practice Direction which fleshes out the detail of the rules. For a further, more detailed discussion of the rules see Patricia Pearl, Small Claims (EMIS Professional Publishing).

Perhaps more significantly in the long term funding or assistance might be available from the Disability Rights Commission, which will go to redress the balance.

The actual rules themselves are relatively straightforward and in reality most District Judges will dispose of two or three Small Claims Track cases in an afternoon.

SUMMARY

- Civil proceedings are limited in scope due to problems with funding and the modest nature of such claims.
- The majority of civil claims will be allocated to the Small Claims Track due to a likely limited award of quantum.
- Scope exists for cases to be allocated to other tracks and in appropriate cases there exists the scope to bring group litigation.
- The rules which will govern the bulk of such claims are to be found in Part 27 of the Civil Procedure Rules.
- The existence of the Disability Rights Commission might enhance the role that civil proceedings have enjoyed to date.

CHAPTER FOURTEEN
REMEDIES IN THE COUNTY COURT

SYNOPSIS

If a claim is brought successfully in the county court, consideration should be given to remedies. In essence any remedy that would normally be available can be awarded in a disability discrimination case and accordingly there is scope for remedies additional to damages to be sought.

THE CONCEPTS

The full panoply of county court remedies are available in Part III proceedings (section 25(5) DDA 1995):

> (5) The remedies available in such proceedings are those which are available in the High Court or (as the case may be) the Court of Session.

DECLARATIONS

In an appropriate case, a declaration might be sought as to the respective rights of the parties. This will be of limited significance in most cases though.

INJUNCTIONS

Of more significance might be an application for an injunction, requiring a defendant to cease carrying on with a discriminatory practice or conversely to take positive steps by a mandatory injunction to remedy a state of affairs which constitutes discrimination.

DAMAGES

The measure of compensation for tortious injury, is that measure which is required to put the injured victim into the same position they would have been in had the tort not occurred. In the context of DDA 1995 claims however, a further head of damage is recognised, which is not generally recoverable in the law of tort. This is injury to feelings (section 25(2) DDA 1995):

> (2) For the avoidance of doubt, it is hereby declared that damages in respect of discrimination in a way which is unlawful under this Part may include compensation for injury to feelings whether or not they include compensation under any other head.

STRATEGIC CONSIDERATIONS

Most actions will be for damages. But where appropriate other remedies can be sought. Special damages can be claimed, subject to the normal rules of remoteness which apply to tortious actions.

Injury to feelings does not carry a prescribed tariff. But reference can and should be made to the *Judicial Studies Board Guidelines (5th edition)* which apply to psychiatric injury and will provide some guidance as to the sort of figure which would apply to a mental injury, as opposed to hurt feelings. In addition, see tables of actual damages awards in *Employment Law & Litigation* (EMIS Professional Publishing).

SUMMARY

- Any remedy available on a final hearing in the county court can be sought in disability discrimination proceedings.
- The remedies which will principally be sought will be declarations, injunctions and damages.
- Injunctions can be sought which are prohibitory in nature or mandatory depending on the claimant's complaint.
- Most awards of damages will be limited to injury to feelings but special damages can be claimed too.

- Reference should be had to the *Judicial Studies Board Guidelines (5th edition)* relevant to psychiatric injuries in assessing the value of any claim for injuries to feelings.

CHAPTER FIFTEEN VICTIMISATION AND OTHER PROVISIONS

SYNOPSIS

The concept of victimisation together with related provisions for vicarious liability are now considered briefly in this chapter, which concludes the study of the role of the DDA 1995 in disability discrimination litigation.

THE CONCEPTS

Certain provisions in the DDA 1995 are applicable both to Part II and Part III claims. The most important of these relates to victimisation, which if raised and found to have occurred may constitute discrimination and permit a finding that the complainant has been discriminated against, even if the primary cause of action based on less favourable treatment or a failure to comply with a section 6 or section 21 duty is misplaced.

VICTIMISATION

Section 55 of the DDA 1995 provides that a person discriminates against another if he treats him less favourably than he treats or would treat other persons whose circumstances are the same as that person's for a reason specified in the Act. The reasons are:

- The person has brought proceedings against the alleged discriminator or any other person under the Act.
- The person has given evidence or information in connection with such proceedings brought by any person.

- The person has otherwise done anything under the DDA 1995 in relation to the person responsible for the less favourable treatment or anyone else.
- The person has alleged that the person responsible for the less favourable treatment has contravened the DDA 1995, whether the allegation so states or not.
- The person responsible for the less favourable treatment believes that person has done or intends to do any of those things.

A person will only lose the protection of this section if the allegation made by them is false and not made in good faith (section 55(4) DDA 1995).

EMPLOYERS, EMPLOYEES, PRINCIPALS AND AGENTS

Who will be the respondent to litigation? In most cases it will plainly be the employer or the commercial organisation alleged to have committed the act of less favourable treatment or failed to take reasonable adjustments. These may be the most obvious respondents and will probably be the only ones with relatively deep pockets. But the ambit of the Act is wider than this and allows "accomplices" and the employees or agents whose actions make the employer or principal vicariously liable to be joined to proceedings as well.

Section 57 of the DDA 1995 provides:

> (1) A person who knowingly aids another person to do an act made unlawful by this Act is to be treated for the purposes of this Act as himself doing the same kind of unlawful act.
>
> (2) For the purposes of this subsection (1), an employee or agent for whose act the employer or principal is liable under section 58 (or would be so liable but for section 58(5)) shall be taken to have aided the employer or principal to do the act.

This is supplemented by a defence available to the employee or agent, however.

> (3) For the purposes of this section, a person does not knowingly aid another to do an unlawful act if –
>
> (a) he acts in reliance on a statement made to him by that other person that, because of any provision of this Act, the act would not be unlawful; and
>
> (b) it is reasonable for him to rely on the statement.

It should be noted that should this defence be made out, namely that someone committed an act of discrimination because they were told by a third party that this was lawful under the DDA 1995, that third party will have committed a criminal offence punishable by a fine in the Magistrates' Court (section 57(4)-(5) DDA 1995.

VICARIOUS LIABILITY

Disability discrimination is a statutory tort. Accordingly, as with any other tort, if it is committed by an employee or agent acting in the course of his employment or with his principal's authority, that will serve to make the employer or principal vicariously liable for the tort. It is crucial that in the context of the employee's tort, he is acting in the course of his employment and not engaged on a frolic of his own. In relation to an agent, it should be noted that the authority can be express or implied.

The employer or principal, can make use of a statutory defence of "reasonable practicability" in order to effectively dissociate the employer or principal from the discriminatory act:

> (4) In proceedings under this Act against any person in respect of an act alleged to have been done by an employee of his, it shall be a defence for that person to prove that he took such steps as were reasonably practicable to prevent the employee from –
> (a) doing that act; or
> (b) doing, in the course of his employment, acts of that description.

In effect there would then be a claim against two respondents, both of whose response might be markedly different.

STRATEGIC CONSIDERATIONS

Two points are of particular significance in relation to these provisions. The first is that victimisation can often overshadow or overtake a claim which itself may be ill-founded, but which will afford a remedy where the complainant has had action taken against him for daring to consider or to carry out a protected act.

The second point is in relation to vicarious liability. In most discrimination claims, where a company or principal is seen as the respondent or defendant to litigation, the company does not necessarily fall because of the actions of one bigoted employee or agent. The company or principal can rely on a defence of reasonable practicability to dissociate from the employee or agent. In such circumstances consideration must be given to whether more than one party should be joined as tortfeasor, and of course a reliance on the reasonable practicability defence will raise a conflict between the employee or agent and employer or principal.

SUMMARY

- Victimisation can arise after proceedings have begun and a claim for discrimination on this ground should be raised by way of amendment.
- When allegations of disability discrimination are raised, the employer or service provider must be very careful that their actions or subsequent treatment of the complainant cannot be interpreted as victimisation.
- Principles of vicarious liability are contained within the DDA 1995 and accordingly consideration must be given to whom is the proper respondent or defendant to proceedings.
- Otherwise blameless employers or principals can raise a reasonable practicability defence in an attempt to dissociate themselves from a tortfeasor whose actions they would otherwise be responsible for.
- Such dissociation raises a conflict of interest between the two parties.

CHAPTER SIXTEEN
THE HUMAN RIGHTS ACT 1998 AND THE EUROPEAN CONVENTION OF HUMAN RIGHTS

SYNOPSIS

The HRA 1998 potentially opens a new front in disability discrimination litigation. But the Act introduces concepts unfamiliar to domestic lawyers and it remains unclear how great an impact the Act will have in practical terms. This chapter considers the principal provisions of the statute.

THE CONCEPTS

The HRA 1998 is intended to give effect in domestic law to the rights secured under the European Convention on Human Rights. This international treaty was ratified by the United Kingdom, but under a dualist system of international law could not be relied upon directly in this country. The HRA 1998 could have a profound effect in providing redress and enforceable rights to disabled people, if used inventively and with thought.

The European Convention for the Protection of Human Rights and Fundamental Freedoms is an international treaty of the Council of Europe. It was adopted in 1950, ratified by the UK in 1951 and came into force in 1953.

The Convention has three sections:

- Section I: a list of rights and freedoms.
- Section II: the establishment of the European Court of Human Rights
- Section III: miscellaneous provisions.

The UK has thus been signed up to the *international* treaty for almost half a century. Despite being an international agreement, which put obligations on the UK Government, the Convention did not and was not part of the UK's domestic law. Thus the courts had no power to enforce the Convention rights directly. If the Convention Rights conflicted with the UK law, then the UK law prevailed. The courts could take indirect notice of the Convention in a number of ways:

- *Resolving ambiguities* If an Act of Parliament or a statutory instrument was ambiguous in its wording, the courts would apply the interpretation, which favoured the Convention Rights.
- *New law* Where the common law, that is the law created by the courts was ambiguous or non existent, the courts could and should consider the Convention in developing the law.
- *Judicial discretion* The courts have held that when considering when or whether to exercise their discretion, judges should take the Convention into account.
- *Judicial review proceedings.*

But this was increasingly seen as inadequate, or not going far enough to ensure that all subjects of this nation had adequate resource to and protection from the State, through a strong declaration of their rights as human beings.

The HRA 1998 was passed in that year and came into force in October 2000. The two year delay, was an attempt to avoid massive compensation claims by the government, who realised many aspects of the way government is run in this country and the laws that exist, would breach Convention Rights.

The 1998 Act is not a written constitution, such as exists in the USA. The courts will not say that Acts of Parliament that conflict with human rights are unconstitutional, nor will they have powers to strike down Acts of Parliament. The judges will remain subject to Parliament, rather than being raised above it.

The Act of 1998 works in the following way:

- All legislation, Acts of Parliament, statutes going back to Magna Carta and beyond must now be interpreted so as to be compatible with the Convention **so far as it is possible to do so** (section 3(1)).

- Subordinate legislation, regulations and the like can be struck down as being incompatible. If Acts of Parliament are found to be incompatible, then the superior Courts, can issued declarations of incompatibility, which are intended to provide a clear signal to Parliament that the Act is in conflict with the Convention and should be amended or repealed (sections 4 and 10(4)).
- It becomes unlawful for public authorities to act in a way which is incompatible with the Convention (section 6).
- Individuals can sue **public authorities** directly for infringing their human rights or rely on Convention rights in proceedings brought against them, by others (section 7).
- Convention rights can be deployed in any court or tribunal proceedings (section 7).
- Convention rights are a bedrock, on which other already existing rights can be supported. The intention of the Act is not to limit people only to the rights in the Convention (section 11).

Private individuals who do not fall within the scope of being a public authority do not escape the Act, as it will be relevant in three ways:

- The state is actively obliged to provide protection for the Convention Rights. Oppression of them by a private individual, due to a failure on the state's part can lead to the state being liable.
- Courts as public authorities will have to develop the common law to ensure that it is compatible with Convention rights.
- Convention rights can be relied upon in any proceedings.

The actual rights which are protected by the Convention are in the main described in section 1. But the rights and what they actually mean have been laid down and interpreted by the European Court on Human Rights in numerous cases over the last 50 years. Accordingly, regard must be had to the law reports to see what the rights actually mean. It should be noted that although the Strasbourg jurisprudence must be taken into account (section 2(1) HRA 1998), by courts and tribunals when determining human rights points, it is not binding upon them. Neither is statutory recognition given to human rights jurisprudence in other jurisdictions, although if based on Convention rights this may be both illuminating and persuasive. It should be noted however that the 21st century is a very different milieu to the 1950s and as society and attitudes change, the ECHR is meant to change and develop too, which would predicate that old decisions grounded in the mores of a particular period might have to be disregarded or given little weight. For regular reporting of Human Rights cases, see *Human Rights and UK Practice* (EMIS Professional Publishing).

THE RIGHTS PROTECTED UNDER THE EUROPEAN CONVENTION

Particular rights will be of significance to disabled people. The most significant are identified below:

Article 2

> Everyone's right to life shall be protected by law. No one shall be deprived of his life intentionally save in the execution of a sentence of a court following his conviction of a crime for which this penalty is provided by law.

Supplemented by *Optional Protocol No 6*

> The death penalty shall be abolished. No one shall be condemned to such penalty or executed.
>
> A state may make provision in its law for the death penalty in respect of acts committed in time of war or of imminent war; such penalty shall be applied only in the instances laid down in the law and in accordance with its provisions...

This right is framed in absolute terms and accordingly is a right which is at the apex of the hierarchy of rights.

Article 3

> No one shall be subjected to torture or to inhuman or degrading treatment or punishment.

Again this right is an absolute right, which would have precedence over other qualified rights.

Article 6

> In the determination of his civil rights and obligations or of any criminal charge against him, everyone is entitled to a fair and public

hearing within a reasonable time by an independent and impartial tribunal established by law. Judgment shall be pronounced publicly but the press and public may be excluded from all or part of the trial in the interests of morals, public order or national security in a democratic society, where the interests of juveniles or the protection of the private life of the parties so require, or to the extent strictly necessary in the opinion of the court in special circumstances where publicity would prejudice the interests of justice.

Article 6 is the so-called right to a fair trial, but it goes beyond simple court proceedings to encompass all determinations of a person's rights.

Article 8

(1) Everyone has the right to respect for his private and family life, his home and his correspondence.

(2) There shall be no interference by a public authority with the exercise of this right except such as is in accordance with the law and is necessary in a democratic society in the interests of national security, public safety or the economic well being of the country, for the prevention of disorder or crime, for the protection of health or morals, or for the protection of the rights and freedoms of others.

Article 8 is the right to respect for one's private life, upon which a nascent common law right to privacy may be developing.

Article 10

(1) Everyone has the right to freedom of expression. This right shall include freedom to hold opinions and to receive and impart information and ideas without interference by public authority and regardless of frontiers. This Article shall not prevent States from requiring the licensing of broadcasting, television or cinema enterprises.

(2) The exercise of these freedoms, since it carries with it duties and responsibilities, may be subject to such formalities, conditions, restrictions or penalties as are prescribed by law and are necessary in a democratic society...

Article 10 is concerned with freedom of speech, but goes beyond this to deal with the receipt of information.

Article 12

> Men and women of marriageable age have the right to marry and to found a family, according to the national laws governing the exercise of this right.

Article 12 is concerned with the rights of individuals to marry and to reproduce.

Article 14

> The enjoyment of the rights and freedoms set forth in this Convention shall be secured without discrimination on any ground such as sex, race, colour, language, religion, political or other opinion, national or social origin, association with a national minority, property, birth or other status.

Article 14 is the anti-discrimination provision that does not stand alone but must be read in conjunction with other rights.

Article 1 of the First Protocol

> Every natural or legal person is entitled to the peaceful enjoyment of his possessions. No one shall be deprived of his possessions except in the public interest and subject to the conditions provided for by law and by the general principles of international law. The preceding provision shall not however, in any way impair the right of a state to enforce such laws, as it deems necessary to control the use of property in accordance with the general interest or to secure the payment of taxes or other contributions or penalties.

Article 1 of the First Protocol, is concerned with the right to enjoyment of property.

STRATEGIC CONSIDERATIONS

The rights protected under the ECHR consist of a number of passages of text, some framed in absolute terms, others subject to derogations and exceptions but all written in very generalised language. The immediate question that any court must grapple with is whether a particular complaint falls within the ambit of a protected right and must be afforded a remedy. This inevitably involves consideration of the right, against the backdrop of decided case law and due to the vast scope of human activity, from broad principles.

Three types of rights can be identified:

- Absolute rights – these cannot be restricted.
- Derogable rights – these permit a state to depart from their otherwise unqualified nature.
- Qualified rights – these require consideration of the broad terms of the rights against a number of restrictions or limitations.

Absolute rights cannot be restricted. Derogable rights permit a state to depart from their otherwise unqualified nature. Qualified rights require consideration of the broad terms of the rights against a number of restrictions or limitations.

In general terms the ECHR is to be interpreted purposively, in order to give to people practical and effective rights, rather than theoretical or illusory ones. This has involved the European Court developing a systematic approach to interpretation of the various rights which looks at issues of state responsibility and positive obligations. It is this question of positive obligations which is of crucial importance if the HRA 1998 is to become a vehicle for advancing the position of disabled people within society. It is not enough, for example, to prohibit discrimination against disabled people on public transport, if they cannot get to the public transport station, cannot read the timetable provided, or cannot climb onto the transport.

The rights protected under the ECHR do not operate in a vacuum. They are subject to restrictions permitted under the Convention expressly and also by the principle of proportionality. Proportionality in this context will also apply to the consideration of restrictions imposed on Convention rights and also to the scope of positive obligations that can be read into the Convention.

When a limitation is imposed on a Convention right, the court will have to look at the proportionality of the restriction. It will consider whether the reasons for restricting the right can be regarded as just and sufficient or whether there are less restrictive alternatives. It will consider whether procedural fairness was exercised and whether in fact the restriction on a right was so extensive in effectively extinguished the right it sought to limit. Consideration of these factors will enable a court to decide whether in fact the restriction is disproportionate and a breach of the Convention

There is no general theory of positive obligations. But Convention rights are framed largely in negative terms; don't kill, don't torture, don't imprison (arbitrarily) and the like. For effective and practical rights to exist, though, positive obligations are implied into particular rights. Thus there can be a duty on state authorities to put into place a legal framework, or to act to prevent breaches of Convention rights particularly where absolute rights or particular interests such as private and family life are at stake. States can also be required to ensure that individuals have information relevant to the exercise of their rights and to provide resources to individuals to prevent breaches of their Convention rights.

SUMMARY

- The HRA 1998 opens a new chapter in disability discrimination and disability rights litigation.
- The HRA 1998 operates in a number of ways but direct claims against public authorities may prove the most fruitful form of litigation permissible under the Act.
- Consideration must be given to human rights jurisprudence, which adds flesh to the bare bones of the Convention rights.
- Positive obligations implied into Convention rights are likely to be the most significant rights for disabled people.
- The hierarchy of rights will create difficulties for courts balancing rights and questions of proportionality.

CHAPTER SEVENTEEN
UTILISING THE HUMAN RIGHTS ACT 1998 IN DISABILITY DISCRIMINATION LITIGATION

SYNOPSIS

This chapter attempts to consider how human rights arguments might be deployed in civil proceedings in the context of disability discrimination litigation.

THE CONCEPTS

The key provision of the Human Rights Act 1998 which will affect disabled people is in regulating their relations with the state and public authorities, is the right to take proceedings against public authorities for damages for compensation or other remedies to protect their human rights which are being infringed or dealt with in a way that is discriminatory.

Section 7 HRA 1998 provides:

> (1) A person who claims that a public authority has acted (or proposes to act) in a way which is made unlawful by section 6(1) may –
> (a) bring proceedings against the authority under this Act in the appropriate court or tribunal, or
> (b) rely on the Convention right or rights concerned in any legal proceedings,
>
> but only if he is or would be a victim of the unlawful act.

If a disabled person wishes to bring a claim for alleged infringement of a right, this section enables a claim to be brought and potentially a remedy granted. But a number of points should be borne in mind:

- Claims can be brought against public authorities. These include courts or tribunals and any person whose functions are of a public nature. This does not include bodies or persons if the nature of the act is private (section 6, HRA 1998).
- A person will only be a victim of the unlawful act, if they would satisfy the test applied by article 34 of the ECHR on who is a victim for the purposes of proceedings in the European Court (section 6(7) HRA 1998).

Proceedings under subsection (1)(a) must be brought within either a year beginning with the date when the act took place or a longer period if the court considers that would be equitable in all the circumstances, but subject to any shorter limitation periods, such as the three month provision for judicial review (section 7(5) HRA 1998).

STRATEGIC CONSIDERATIONS

The procedure for taking action is thus relatively simple. But what sort of case could be brought under these provisions which would materially affect a disabled person's rights and add in a positive way to his or her life?

A number of examples follow:

(1) An NHS trust refuses to give to disabled person a heart transplant, on the basis that the Trust has limited resources and the quality of life of the disabled person is not such that that person should have priority over non-disabled people. Without the operation the disabled person will die.

It can be argued that an action for a mandatory injunction for a heart transplant can be brought grounded on articles 2 and 14, for proposed breach of the right to life and discrimination.

(2) A disabled person is kept in residential accommodation run by a local authority in appalling conditions. The disabled person is charged for the privilege.

An action for breach of article 3, for breach of the right not to suffer degrading treatment can be brought.

(3) Disabled children live in a residential home where they are systematically abused. Despite complaints over the years a supervising local authority fails to investigate or take steps.

An action for damages for breach of article 3, for the right not to suffer torture or inhuman or degrading treatment can be brought against the local authority.

(4) A disabled person applies for social security benefits and the determination of his application is delayed for eighteen months.

An action for damages for breach of article 6, due to excessive delays can be brought.

(5) A deaf person requires sign language tuition or the provision of a communication board. The local authority refuses to provide these aids.

An action for damages might be brought for breach either of article 8 or article 10.

SUMMARY

- The HRA 1998 creates statutory tort by which disabled people can and will assert infringements of their rights by public authorities in civil proceedings.
- Claims can only be made against public authorities and by those who fall within the victim test, who have standing to bring a claim.
- The time limit for such proceedings is short at one year or less.
- Possible test cases can already be discerned.
- Actions in the context of the abuse of absolute rights possess the greatest likelihood of success.

CHAPTER EIGHTEEN

REMEDIES UNDER THE HUMAN RIGHTS ACT 1998

SYNOPSIS

What remedies will the HRA 1998 afford litigants in practical terms? Remedies which can be given are the full panoply of remedies in civil proceedings which include damages, declarations, injunctions. This chapter looks briefly at these remedies.

THE CONCEPTS

A claim brought under section 7(1) which is proved to be well founded can attract any of the normal remedies in court proceedings. Section 8 HRA 1998 provides:

(1) In relation to any act (or proposed act) of a public authority which the court finds is (or would be) unlawful, it may grant such relief or remedy, or make such order, within its powers as it considers just and appropriate.

(2) But damages may be awarded only by a court which has power to award damages, or to order the payment of compensation in civil proceedings.

(3) No award of damages is to be made unless, taking into account all the circumstances of the case, including-
   (a) any other relief or remedy granted, or order made, in relation to the act in question (by that or any other court), and
   (b) the consequences of any decision (of that or any other court) in respect of that act,

   the court is satisfied that the award is necessary to afford just satisfaction to the person in whose favour it is made.

A further qualification is applied in respect of the determination of quantum (section 8(4) HRA 1998):

> (4) In determining –
> (a) whether to award damages, or
> (b) the amount of an award,
> the court must take into account the principles applied by the European Court of Human Rights in relation to the award of compensation under article 41 of the Convention.

It follows that when considering any measure of damages, in effect a European approach will be imported into domestic proceedings by the mechanism of the Act.

Article 41 provides:

> If the Court finds that there has been a violation of the Convention or the protocols thereto, and if the internal law of the High Contracting Party concerned allows only partial reparation to be made, the Court shall, if necessary, afford just satisfaction to the injured party.

The most valuable survey on the approach taken by the European Court, is probably that contained in the recent Law Commission Report (No. 266).

This report makes it plain at Part III that the approach to such damages is not straightforward. A number of problems can be identified. The first of these is the absence of clear principles as to when damages should be awarded and how they should be measured. This draws from differing legal traditions: England and Wales have very detailed law relating to causation and the assessment of damage. France, for example, does not, including considerations of fairness as well as causal potency.

In essence the first hurdle of a three stage test must be met.

- The court must have found a violation.
- The domestic law of the State must allow only partial reparation.
- The award must be necessary to afford just satisfaction.

If those requirements are met, the general approach of the European Court seems to be to order damages on the basis of *restitutio in integrum*.

Heads of damage which can be recovered include, pecuniary loss, non-pecuniary loss and costs and expenses. Awards have been made in respect of pecuniary loss which include loss of earnings, loss of pension rights, medical expenses, unlawfully expropriated property and the re-imbursement of fines.

Non-pecuniary awards have included compensation for pain, suffering and psychological harm, distress, frustration, inconvenience, humiliation and anxiety as well as loss of reputation and even loss of relationship.

Costs and expenses are awarded when they were incurred to prevent or obtain redress and must have been actually incurred and be reasonable in amount.

STRATEGIC CONSIDERATIONS

The domestic courts can award any remedy they could in other proceedings. Applications can be made for injunctions, declarations and also claims for compensation. Where compensation is sought, the practice of the Strasbourg court is brought into play.

The European Convention on Human Rights affords "just satisfaction" to injured parties through article 41. The issue of compensation for the European Court is one where it may exercise its discretion, having regard to what is equitable.

Just satisfaction can be awarded under three heads; pecuniary loss, non-pecuniary loss and costs and expenses. Interest is also payable on these awards.

The Law Commission has recently published a paper on damages in human rights cases, and recourse should be had to this paper when advising on potential awards of damages. But there should be considerable scope for arguing in respect of disability discrimination claims that compensation should include sizeable awards for non-pecuniary loss.

SUMMARY

- The full range of civil remedies can be awarded in civil proceedings.
- A court which does not have the power to award damages cannot award them.
- Regard should be had to the case-law on the European Convention of Human Rights to determine the attitude of the European Court of Human Rights to questions of compensation.
- The approach of domestic courts to compensation should mirror that of the European Court of Human Rights.
- The Law Commission's paper on damages in human rights cases is useful reading on the approach likely to be taken by domestic courts.

APPENDIX
THE DISABILITY DISCRIMINATION ACT 1995 AND SCHEDULES

DISABILITY DISCRIMINATION ACT 1995

ARRANGEMENT OF SECTIONS

Part III
Discrimination in Other Areas
Goods, facilities and services

19. Discrimination in relation to goods, facilities and services
20. Meaning of "discrimination"
21. Duty of providers of services to make adjustments

Premises

22. Discrimination in relation to premises
23. Exemption for small dwellings
24. Meaning of "discrimination"

Enforcement, etc.

25. Enforcement, remedies and procedure
26. Validity and revision of certain agreements
27. Alterations to premises occupied under leases
28. Advice and assistance

Part IV
Education

29. Education of disabled persons
30. Further and higher education of disabled persons
31. Further and higher education of disabled persons: Scotland

Part V
Public Transport
Taxis

32. Taxi accessibility regulations
33. Designated transport facilities
34. New licences conditional on compliance with taxi accessibility regulations
35. Exemption from taxi accessibility regulations.
36. Carrying of passengers in wheelchairs
37. Carrying of guide dogs and hearing dogs
38. Appeal against refusal of exemption certificate
39. Requirements as to disabled passengers in Scotland

Public service vehicles – PSV accessibility regulations

41. Accessibility certificates
42. Approval certificates
43. Special authorisations
44. Reviews and appeals
45. Fees

Rail vehicles

46. Rail vehicle accessibility regulations
47. Exemption from rail vehicle accessibility regulations.

Supplemental

48. Offences by bodies corporate etc
49. Forgery and false statements

Part VI

The National Disability Council

50. The National Disability Council
51. Codes of practice prepared by the Council
52. Further provision about codes issued under section 51

Part VII

Supplemental

53. Codes of practice prepared by the Secretary of State
54. Further provision about codes issued under section 53
55. Victimisation
56. Help for persons suffering discrimination
57. Aiding unlawful acts
58. Liability of employers and principals
59. Statutory authority and national security etc

Part VIII

Miscellaneous

60. Appointment by Secretary of State of advisers
61. Amendment of Disabled Persons (Employment) Act 1944
62. Restriction of publicity: industrial tribunals
63. Restriction of publicity: Employment Appeal Tribunal
64. Application to Crown etc
65. Application to Parliament
66. Government appointments outside Part II
67. Regulations and orders
68. Interpretation
69. Financial provisions
70. Short title, commencement, extent etc

SCHEDULES

Schedule 1 – Provisions Supplementing Section 1

Schedule 2 – Past Disabilities

Schedule 3 – Enforcement and Procedure

Part I – Employment

Part II – Discrimination in Other Areas

Schedule 4 – Premises Occupied Under Leases

Part I – Occupation by Employer or Trade Organisation

Part II – Occupation by Provider of Services

Schedule 5 – The National Disability Council

Schedule 6 – Consequential Amendments

Schedule 7 – Repeals

Schedule 8 – Modifications of this Act in its Application to Northern Ireland

The Text of the Act

An Act to make it unlawful to discriminate against disabled persons in connection with employment, the provision of goods, facilities and services or the disposal or management of premises; to make provision about the employment of disabled persons; and to establish a National Disability Council.

8th November 1995

Be it enacted by the Queen's most Excellent Majesty, by and with the advice and consent of the Lords Spiritual and Temporal, and Commons, in this present Parliament assembled, and by the authority of the same, as follows: –

PART I
Disability

Meaning of "disability" and "disabled person"

1. (1) Subject to the provisions of Schedule 1, a person has a disability for the purposes of this Act if he has a physical or mental impairment which has a substantial and long-term adverse effect on his ability to carry out normal day-to-day activities.

(2) In this Act "disabled person" means a person who has a disability.

Past disabilities

2. (1) The provisions of this Part and Parts II and III apply in relation to a person who has had a disability as they apply in relation to a person who has that disability.

(2) Those provisions are subject to the modifications made by Schedule 2.

(3) Any regulations or order made under this Act may include provision with respect to persons who have had a disability.

(4) In any proceedings under Part II or Part III of this Act, the question whether a person had a disability at a particular time ("the relevant time") shall be determined, for the purposes of this section, as if the provisions of, or made under, this Act in force when the act complained of was done had been in force at the relevant time.

(5) The relevant time may be a time before the passing of this Act.

Guidance

3. (1) The Secretary of State may issue guidance about the matters to be taken into account in determining –

(a) whether an impairment has a substantial adverse effect on a person's ability to carry out normal day-to-day activities; or

(b) whether such an impairment has a long-term effect.

(2) The guidance may, among other things, give examples of –

(a) effects which it would be reasonable, in relation to particular activities, to regard for purposes of this Act as substantial adverse effects;

(b) effects which it would not be reasonable, in relation to particular activities, to regard for such purposes as substantial adverse effects;

(c) substantial adverse effects which it would be reasonable to regard, for such purposes, as long-term;

(d) substantial adverse effects which it would not be reasonable to regard, for such purposes, as long-term.

(3) A tribunal or court determining, for any purpose of this Act, whether an impairment has a substantial and long-term adverse effect on a person's ability to carry out normal day-to-day activities, shall take into account any guidance which appears to it to be relevant.

(4) In preparing a draft of any guidance, the Secretary of State shall consult such persons as he considers appropriate.

(5) Where the Secretary of State proposes to issue any guidance, he shall publish a draft of it, consider any representations that are made to him about the draft and, if he thinks it appropriate, modify his proposals in the light of any of those representations.

(6) If the Secretary of State decides to proceed with any proposed guidance, he shall lay a draft of it before each House of Parliament.

(7) If, within the 40-day period, either House resolves not to approve the draft, the Secretary of State shall take no further steps in relation to the proposed guidance.

(8) If no such resolution is made within the 40-day period, the Secretary of State shall issue the guidance in the form of his draft.

(9) The guidance shall come into force on such date as the Secretary of State may appoint by order.

(10) Subsection (7) does not prevent a new draft of the proposed guidance from being laid before Parliament.

(11) The Secretary of State may –

(a) from time to time revise the whole or part of any guidance and re-issue it;
(b) by order revoke any guidance.

(12) In this section –

"40-day period", in relation to the draft of any proposed guidance, means –

(a) if the draft is laid before one House on a day later than the day on which it is laid before the other House, the period of 40 days beginning with the later of the two days, and
(b) in any other case, the period of 40 days beginning with the day on which the draft is laid before each House,

no account being taken of any period during which Parliament is dissolved or prorogued or during which both Houses are adjourned for more than 4 days; and

"guidance" means guidance issued by the Secretary of State under this section and includes guidance which has been revised and re-issued.

PART II

Employment

Discrimination by employers

Discrimination against applicants and employees

4. (1) It is unlawful for an employer to discriminate against a disabled person –

(a) in the arrangements which he makes for the purpose of determining to whom he should offer employment;
(b) in the terms on which he offers that person employment; or

(c) by refusing to offer, or deliberately not offering, him employment.

(2) It is unlawful for an employer to discriminate against a disabled person whom he employs –
(a) in the terms of employment which he affords him;
(b) in the opportunities which he affords him for promotion, a transfer, training or receiving any other benefit;
(c) by refusing to afford him, or deliberately not affording him, any such opportunity; or
(d) by dismissing him, or subjecting him to any other detriment.

(3) Subsection (2) does not apply to benefits of any description if the employer is concerned with the provision (whether or not for payment) of benefits of that description to the public, or to a section of the public which includes the employee in question, unless –
(a) that provision differs in a material respect from the provision of the benefits by the employer to his employees; or
(b) the provision of the benefits to the employee in question is regulated by his contract of employment; or
(c) the benefits relate to training.

(4) In this Part "benefits" includes facilities and services.

(5) In the case of an act which constitutes discrimination by virtue of section 55, this section also applies to discrimination against a person who is not disabled.

(6) This section applies only in relation to employment at an establishment in Great Britain.

Meaning of "discrimination"

5. (1) For the purposes of this Part, an employer discriminates against a disabled person if –
(a) for a reason which relates to the disabled person's disability, he treats him less favourably than he treats or would treat others to whom that reason does not or would not apply; and
(b) he cannot show that the treatment in question is justified.

(2) For the purposes of this Part, an employer also discriminates against a disabled person if –
(a) he fails to comply with a section 6 duty imposed on him in relation to the disabled person; and
(b) he cannot show that his failure to comply with that duty is justified.

(3) Subject to subsection (5), for the purposes of subsection (1) treatment is justified if, but only if, the reason for it is both material to the circumstances of the particular case and substantial.

(4) For the purposes of subsection (2), failure to comply with a section 6 duty is justified if, but only if, the reason for the failure is both material to the circumstances of the particular case and substantial.

(5) If, in a case falling within subsection (1), the employer is under a section 6 duty in relation to the disabled person but fails without justification to comply with that duty, his treatment of that person cannot be justified under subsection (3) unless it would have been justified even if he had complied with the section 6 duty.

(6) Regulations may make provision, for purposes of this section, as to circumstances in which –
(a) treatment is to be taken to be justified;
(b) failure to comply with a section 6 duty is to be taken to be justified;
(c) treatment is to be taken not to be justified;
(d) failure to comply with a section 6 duty is to be taken not to be justified.

(7) Regulations under subsection (6) may, in particular –
(a) make provision by reference to the cost of affording any benefit; and
(b) in relation to benefits under occupational pension schemes, make provision with a view to enabling uniform rates of contributions to be maintained.

Duty of employer to make adjustments

6. (1) Where –
(a) any arrangements made by or on behalf of an employer, or
(b) any physical feature of premises occupied by the employer

place the disabled person concerned at a substantial disadvantage in comparison with persons who are not disabled, it is the duty of the employer to take such steps as it is reasonable, in all the circumstances of the case, for him to have to take in order to prevent the arrangements or feature having that effect.

(2) Subsection (1)(a) applies only in relation to –
(a) arrangements for determining to whom employment should be offered;
(b) any term, condition or arrangements on which employment, promotion, a transfer, training or any other benefit is offered or afforded.

(3) The following are examples of steps which an employer may have to take in relation to a disabled person in order to comply with subsection (1) –
(a) making adjustments to premises;
(b) allocating some of the disabled person's duties to another person;
(c) transferring him to fill an existing vacancy;
(d) altering his working hours;
(e) assigning him to a different place of work;
(f) allowing him to be absent during working hours for rehabilitation, assessment or treatment;
(g) giving him, or arranging for him to be given, training;
(h) acquiring or modifying equipment;
(i) modifying instructions or reference manuals;
(j) modifying procedures for testing or assessment;
(k) providing a reader or interpreter;
(l) providing supervision.

(4) In determining whether it is reasonable for an employer to have to take a particular step in order to comply with subsection (1), regard shall be had, in particular, to –
(a) the extent to which taking the step would prevent the effect in question;
(b) the extent to which it is practicable for the employer to take the step;
(c) the financial and other costs which would be incurred by the employer in taking the step and the extent to which taking it would disrupt any of his activities;
(d) the extent of the employer's financial and other resources;

(e) the availability to the employer of financial or other assistance with respect to taking the step.

This subsection is subject to any provision of regulations made under subsection (8).

(5) In this section, "the disabled person concerned" means –

(a) in the case of arrangements for determining to whom employment should be offered, any disabled person who is, or has notified the employer that he may be, an applicant for that employment;

(b) in any other case, a disabled person who is –

(i) an applicant for the employment concerned; or

(ii) an employee of the employer concerned.

(6) Nothing in this section imposes any duty on an employer in relation to a disabled person if the employer does not know, and could not reasonably be expected to know –

(a) in the case of an applicant or potential applicant, that the disabled person concerned is, or may be, an applicant for the employment; or

(b) in any case, that that person has a disability and is likely to be affected in the way mentioned in subsection (1).

(7) Subject to the provisions of this section, nothing in this Part is to be taken to require an employer to treat a disabled person more favourably than he treats or would treat others.

(8) Regulations may make provision, for the purposes of subsection (1) –

(a) as to circumstances in which arrangements are, or a physical feature is, to be taken to have the effect mentioned in that subsection;

(b) as to circumstances in which arrangements are not, or a physical feature is not, to be taken to have that effect;

(c) as to circumstances in which it is reasonable for an employer to have to take steps of a prescribed description;

(d) as to steps which it is always reasonable for an employer to have to take;

(e) as to circumstances in which it is not reasonable for an employer to have to take steps of a prescribed description;

(f) as to steps which it is never reasonable for an employer to have to take;

(g) as to things which are to be treated as physical features;

(h) as to things which are not to be treated as such features.

(9) Regulations made under subsection (8)(c), (d), (e) or (f) may, in particular, make provision by reference to the cost of taking the steps concerned.

(10) Regulations may make provision adding to the duty imposed on employers by this section, including provision of a kind which may be made under subsection (8).

(11) This section does not apply in relation to any benefit under an occupational pension scheme or any other benefit payable in money or money's worth under a scheme or arrangement for the benefit of employees in respect of –

(a) termination of service;

(b) retirement, old age or death;

(c) accident, injury, sickness or invalidity; or

(d) any other prescribed matter.

(12) This section imposes duties only for the purpose of determining whether an employer has discriminated against a disabled person; and accordingly a breach of any such duty is not actionable as such.

Exemption for small businesses

7. (1) Nothing in this Part applies in relation to an employer who has fewer than 20 employees.

(2) The Secretary of State may by order amend subsection (1) by substituting a different number (not greater than 20) for the number for the time being specified there.

(3) In this section –
"anniversary" means the anniversary of the coming into force of this section; and "review" means a review of the effect of this section.

(4) Before making any order under subsection (2), the Secretary of State shall conduct a review.

(5) Unless he has already begun or completed a review under subsection (4), the Secretary of State shall begin to conduct a review immediately after the fourth anniversary.

(6) Any review shall be completed within nine months.

(7) In conducting any review, the Secretary of State shall consult –
- (a) such organisations representing the interests of employers as he considers appropriate; and
- (b) such organisations representing the interests of disabled persons in employment or seeking employment as he considers appropriate.

(8) If, on completing a review, the Secretary of State decides to make an order under subsection (2), he shall make such an order to come into force not later than one year after the commencement of the review.

(9) If, on completing a review, the Secretary of State decides not to make such an order, he shall not later than one year after the commencement of the review lay before Parliament a report –
- (a) summarising the results of the review; and
- (b) giving the reasons for his decision.

(10) Any report made by the Secretary of State under subsection (9) shall include a summary of the views expressed to him in his consultations.

Enforcement, etc

Enforcement, remedies and procedure

8. (1) A complaint by any person that another person –
- (a) has discriminated against him in a way which is unlawful under this Part, or
- (b) is, by virtue of section 57 or 58, to be treated as having discriminated against him in such a way, may be presented to an industrial tribunal.

(2) Where an industrial tribunal finds that a complaint presented to it under this section is well-founded, it shall take such of the following steps as it considers just and equitable –
- (a) making a declaration as to the rights of the complainant and the respondent in relation to the matters to which the complaint relates;
- (b) ordering the respondent to pay compensation to the complainant;
- (c) recommending that the respondent take, within a specified period, action appearing to the tribunal to be reasonable, in all the circumstances of the case, for the purpose of obviating or reducing the

adverse effect on the complainant of any matter to which the complaint relates.

(3) Where a tribunal orders compensation under subsection (2)(b), the amount of the compensation shall be calculated by applying the principles applicable to the calculation of damages in claims in tort or (in Scotland) in reparation for breach of statutory duty.

(4) For the avoidance of doubt it is hereby declared that compensation in respect of discrimination in a way which is unlawful under this Part may include compensation for injury to feelings whether or not it includes compensation under any other head.

(5) If the respondent to a complaint fails, without reasonable justification, to comply with a recommendation made by an industrial tribunal under subsection (2)(c) the tribunal may, if it thinks it just and equitable to do so –

(a) increase the amount of compensation required to be paid to the complainant in respect of the complaint, where an order was made under subsection (2)(b); or

(b) make an order under subsection (2)(b).

(6) Regulations may make provision –

(a) for enabling a tribunal, where an amount of compensation falls to be awarded under subsection (2)(b), to include in the award interest on that amount; and

(b) specifying, for cases where a tribunal decides that an award is to include an amount in respect of interest, the manner in which and the periods and rate by reference to which the interest is to be determined.

(7) Regulations may modify the operation of any order made under paragraph 6A of Schedule 9 to the [1978 c. 44.] Employment Protection (Consolidation) Act 1978 (power to make provision as to interest on sums payable in pursuance of industrial tribunal decisions) to the extent that it relates to an award of compensation under subsection (2)(b).

(8) Part I of Schedule 3 makes further provision about the enforcement of this Part and about procedure.

Validity of certain agreements

9. (1) Any term in a contract of employment or other agreement is void so far as it purports to –

(a) require a person to do anything which would contravene any provision of, or made under, this Part;

(b) exclude or limit the operation of any provision of this Part; or

(c) prevent any person from presenting a complaint to an industrial tribunal under this Part.

(2) Paragraphs (b) and (c) of subsection (1) do not apply to an agreement not to institute proceedings under section 8(1), or to an agreement not to continue such proceedings, if –

(a) a conciliation officer has acted under paragraph 1 of Schedule 3 in relation to the matter; or

(b) the conditions set out in subsection (3) are satisfied.

(3) The conditions are that –

(a) the complainant must have received independent legal advice from a qualified lawyer as to the terms and effect of the proposed agreement (and in particular its effect on his ability to pursue his complaint before an industrial tribunal);

(b) when the adviser gave the advice there must have been in force a policy of insurance covering the risk of a claim by the complainant in respect of loss arising in consequence of the advice; and

(c) the agreement must be in writing, relate to the particular complaint, identify the adviser and state that the conditions are satisfied.

(4) In this section –

"independent", in relation to legal advice to the complainant, means that it is given by a lawyer who is not acting for the other party or for a person who is connected with that other party; and

"qualified lawyer" means –

(a) as respects proceedings in England and Wales, a barrister (whether in practice as such or employed to give legal advice) or a solicitor of the Supreme Court who holds a practising certificate; and

(b) as respects proceedings in Scotland, an advocate (whether in practice as such or employed to give legal advice) or a solicitor who holds a practising certificate.

(5) For the purposes of subsection (4), any two persons are to be treated as connected if –

(a) one is a company of which the other (directly or indirectly) has control, or

(b) both are companies of which a third person (directly or indirectly) has control.

Charities and support for particular groups of persons

10. (1) Nothing in this Part –

(a) affects any charitable instrument which provides for conferring benefits on one or more categories of person determined by reference to any physical or mental capacity; or

(b) makes unlawful any act done by a charity or recognised body in pursuance of any of its charitable purposes, so far as those purposes are connected with persons so determined.

(2) Nothing in this Part prevents –

(a) a person who provides supported employment from treating members of a particular group of disabled persons more favourably than other persons in providing such employment; or

(b) the Secretary of State from agreeing to arrangements for the provision of supported employment which will, or may, have that effect.

(3) In this section –

"charitable instrument" means an enactment or other instrument (whenever taking effect) so far as it relates to charitable purposes;

"charity" has the same meaning as in the [1993 c. 10.] Charities Act 1993;

"recognised body" means a body which is a recognised body for the purposes of Part I of the [1990 c. 40.] Law Reform (Miscellaneous Provisions) (Scotland) Act 1990; and

"supported employment" means facilities provided, or in respect of which payments are made, under section 15 of the [1944 c. 10.] Disabled Persons (Employment) Act 1944.

(4) In the application of this section to England and Wales, "charitable purposes" means purposes which are exclusively charitable according to the law of England and Wales.

(5) In the application of this section to Scotland, "charitable purposes" shall be construed in the same way as if it were contained in the Income Tax Acts.

Advertisements suggesting that employers will discriminate against disabled persons

11. (1) This section applies where –

(a) a disabled person has applied for employment with an employer;

(b) the employer has refused to offer, or has deliberately not offered, him the employment;

(c) the disabled person has presented a complaint under section 8 against the employer;

(d) the employer has advertised the employment (whether before or after the disabled person applied for it); and

(e) the advertisement indicated, or might reasonably be understood to have indicated, that any application for the advertised employment would, or might, be determined to any extent by reference to –

(i) the successful applicant not having any disability or any category of disability which includes the disabled person's disability; or

(ii) the employer's reluctance to take any action of a kind mentioned in section 6.

(2) The tribunal hearing the complaint shall assume, unless the contrary is shown, that the employer's reason for refusing to offer, or deliberately not offering, the employment to the complainant was related to the complainant's disability.

(3) In this section "advertisement" includes every form of advertisement or notice, whether to the public or not.

Discrimination by other persons

Discrimination against contract workers

12. (1) It is unlawful for a principal, in relation to contract work, to discriminate against a disabled person –

(a) in the terms on which he allows him to do that work;

(b) by not allowing him to do it or continue to do it;

(c) in the way he affords him access to any benefits or by refusing or deliberately omitting to afford him access to them; or

(d) by subjecting him to any other detriment.

(2) Subsection (1) does not apply to benefits of any description if the principal is concerned with the provision (whether or not for payment) of benefits of that description to the public, or to a section of the public which includes the contract worker in question, unless that provision differs in a material respect from the provision of the benefits by the principal to contract workers.

(3) The provisions of this Part (other than subsections (1) to (3) of section 4) apply to any principal, in relation to contract work, as if he were, or would be, the employer of the contract worker and as if any contract worker supplied to do work for him were an employee of his.

(4) In the case of an act which constitutes discrimination by virtue of section 55, this section also applies to discrimination against a person who is not disabled.

(5) This section applies only in relation to contract work done at an establishment in Great Britain (the provisions of section 68 about the meaning of "employment at an establishment in Great Britain" applying for the purposes of this subsection with the appropriate modifications).

(6) In this section –
"principal" means a person ("A") who makes work available for doing by individuals who are employed by another person who supplies them under a contract made with A;
"contract work" means work so made available; and
"contract worker" means any individual who is supplied to the principal under such a contract.

Discrimination by trade organisations

13. (1) It is unlawful for a trade organisation to discriminate against a disabled person –
   (a) in the terms on which it is prepared to admit him to membership of the organisation; or
   (b) by refusing to accept, or deliberately not accepting, his application for membership.

(2) It is unlawful for a trade organisation, in the case of a disabled person who is a member of the organisation, to discriminate against him –
   (a) in the way it affords him access to any benefits or by refusing or deliberately omitting to afford him access to them;
   (b) by depriving him of membership, or varying the terms on which he is a member; or
   (c) by subjecting him to any other detriment.

(3) In the case of an act which constitutes discrimination by virtue of section 55, this section also applies to discrimination against a person who is not disabled.

(4) In this section "trade organisation" means an organisation of workers, an organisation of employers or any other organisation whose members carry on a particular profession or trade for the purposes of which the organisation exists.

Meaning of "discrimination" in relation to trade organisations

14. (1) For the purposes of this Part, a trade organisation discriminates against a disabled person if –
   (a) for a reason which relates to the disabled person's disability, it treats him less favourably than it treats or would treat others to whom that reason does not or would not apply; and
   (b) it cannot show that the treatment in question is justified.

(2) For the purposes of this Part, a trade organisation also discriminates against a disabled person if –
   (a) it fails to comply with a section 15 duty imposed on it in relation to the disabled person; and
   (b) it cannot show that its failure to comply with that duty is justified.

(3) Subject to subsection (5), for the purposes of subsection (1) treatment is justified if, but only if, the reason for it is both material to the circumstances of the particular case and substantial.

(4) For the purposes of subsection (2), failure to comply with a section 15 duty is justified if, but only if, the reason for the failure is both material to the circumstances of the particular case and substantial.

(5) If, in a case falling within subsection (1), the trade organisation is under a section 15 duty in relation to the disabled person concerned but fails without justification to comply with that duty, its treatment of that person cannot be justified under subsection (3) unless the treatment would have been justified even if the organisation had complied with the section 15 duty.

(6) Regulations may make provision, for purposes of this section, as to circumstances in which –
- (a) treatment is to be taken to be justified;
- (b) failure to comply with a section 15 duty is to be taken to be justified;
- (c) treatment is to be taken not to be justified;
- (d) failure to comply with a section 15 duty is to be taken not to be justified.

Appeal against refusal of exemption certificate

15. (1) Where –
- (a) any arrangements made by or on behalf of a trade organisation, or
- (b) any physical feature of premises occupied by the organisation, place the disabled person concerned at a substantial disadvantage in comparison with persons who are not disabled, it is the duty of the organisation to take such steps as it is reasonable, in all the circumstances of the case, for it to have to take in order to prevent the arrangements or feature having that effect.

(2) Subsection (1)(a) applies only in relation to –
- (a) arrangements for determining who should become or remain a member of the organisation;
- (b) any term, condition or arrangements on which membership or any benefit is offered or afforded.

(3) In determining whether it is reasonable for a trade organisation to have to take a particular step in order to comply with subsection (1), regard shall be had, in particular, to –
- (a) the extent to which taking the step would prevent the effect in question;
- (b) the extent to which it is practicable for the organisation to take the step;
- (c) the financial and other costs which would be incurred by the organisation in taking the step and the extent to which taking it would disrupt any of its activities;
- (d) the extent of the organisation's financial and other resources;
- (e) the availability to the organisation of financial or other assistance with respect to taking the step.

This subsection is subject to any provision of regulations made under subsection (7).

(4) In this section "the disabled person concerned" means –
- (a) in the case of arrangements for determining to whom membership should be offered, any disabled person who is, or has notified the organisation that he may be, an applicant for membership;
- (b) in any other case, a disabled person who is –

(i) an applicant for membership; or
(ii) a member of the organisation.

(5) Nothing in this section imposes any duty on an organisation in relation to a disabled person if the organisation does not know, and could not reasonably be expected to know that the disabled person concerned –
(a) is, or may be, an applicant for membership; or
(b) has a disability and is likely to be affected in the way mentioned in subsection (1).

(6) Subject to the provisions of this section, nothing in this Part is to be taken to require a trade organisation to treat a disabled person more favourably than it treats or would treat others.

(7) Regulations may make provision for the purposes of subsection (1) as to any of the matters mentioned in paragraphs (a) to (h) of section 6(8) (the references in those paragraphs to an employer being read for these purposes as references to a trade organisation).

(8) Subsection (9) of section 6 applies in relation to such regulations as it applies in relation to regulations made under section 6(8).

(9) Regulations may make provision adding to the duty imposed on trade organisations by this section, including provision of a kind which may be made under subsection (7).

(10) This section imposes duties only for the purpose of determining whether a trade organisation has discriminated against a disabled person; and accordingly a breach of any such duty is not actionable as such.

Premises occupied under leases

Alterations to premises occupied under leases

16. (1) This section applies where –
(a) an employer or trade organisation ("the occupier") occupies premises under a lease;
(b) but for this section, the occupier would not be entitled to make a particular alteration to the premises; and
(c) the alteration is one which the occupier proposes to make in order to comply with a section 6 duty or section 15 duty.

(2) Except to the extent to which it expressly so provides, the lease shall have effect by virtue of this subsection as if it provided –
(a) for the occupier to be entitled to make the alteration with the written consent of the lessor;
(b) for the occupier to have to make a written application to the lessor for consent if he wishes to make the alteration;
(c) if such an application is made, for the lessor not to withhold his consent unreasonably; and
(d) for the lessor to be entitled to make his consent subject to reasonable conditions.

(3) In this section –
"lease" includes a tenancy, sub-lease or sub-tenancy and an agreement for a lease, tenancy, sub-lease or sub-tenancy; and
"sub-lease" and "sub-tenancy" have such meaning as may be prescribed.

(4) If the terms and conditions of a lease –

(a) impose conditions which are to apply if the occupier alters the premises, or

(b) entitle the lessor to impose conditions when consenting to the occupier's altering the premises,

the occupier is to be treated for the purposes of subsection (1) as not being entitled to make the alteration.

(5) Part I of Schedule 4 supplements the provisions of this section.

Occupational pension schemes and insurance services

Occupational pension schemes

17. (1) Every occupational pension scheme shall be taken to include a provision ("a non-discrimination rule") –

(a) relating to the terms on which –

(i) persons become members of the scheme; and

(ii) members of the scheme are treated; and

(b) requiring the trustees or managers of the scheme to refrain from any act or omission which, if done in relation to a person by an employer, would amount to unlawful discrimination against that person for the purposes of this Part.

(2) The other provisions of the scheme are to have effect subject to the non-discrimination rule.

(3) Without prejudice to section 67, regulations under this Part may –

(a) with respect to trustees or managers of occupational pension schemes make different provision from that made with respect to employers; or

(b) make provision modifying the application to such trustees or managers of any regulations made under this Part, or of any provisions of this Part so far as they apply to employers.

(4) In determining, for the purposes of this section, whether an act or omission would amount to unlawful discrimination if done by an employer, any provision made under subsection (3) shall be applied as if it applied in relation to the notional employer.

Insurance services

18. (1) This section applies where a provider of insurance services ("the insurer") enters into arrangements with an employer under which the employer's employees, or a class of his employees –

(a) receive insurance services provided by the insurer; or

(b) are given an opportunity to receive such services.

(2) The insurer is to be taken, for the purposes of this Part, to discriminate unlawfully against a disabled person who is a relevant employee if he acts in relation to that employee in a way which would be unlawful discrimination for the purposes of Part III if –

(a) he were providing the service in question to members of the public; and

(b) the employee was provided with, or was trying to secure the provision of, that service as a member of the public.

(3) In this section –

"insurance services" means services of a prescribed description for the provision of benefits in respect of –

(a) termination of service;

(b) retirement, old age or death;
(c) accident, injury, sickness or invalidity; or
(d) any other prescribed matter; and

"relevant employee" means –

(a) in the case of an arrangement which applies to employees of the employer in question, an employee of his;
(b) in the case of an arrangement which applies to a class of employees of the employer, an employee who is in that class.

(4) For the purposes of the definition of "relevant employee" in subsection (3), "employee" , in relation to an employer, includes a person who has applied for, or is contemplating applying for, employment by that employer or (as the case may be) employment by him in the class in question.

PART III

Discrimination in Other Areas

Goods, facilities and services

Discrimination in relation to goods, facilities and services

19. (1) It is unlawful for a provider of services to discriminate against a disabled person –

(a) in refusing to provide, or deliberately not providing, to the disabled person any service which he provides, or is prepared to provide, to members of the public;
(b) in failing to comply with any duty imposed on him by section 21 in circumstances in which the effect of that failure is to make it impossible or unreasonably difficult for the disabled person to make use of any such service;
(c) in the standard of service which he provides to the disabled person or the manner in which he provides it to him; or
(d) in the terms on which he provides a service to the disabled person.

(2) For the purposes of this section and sections 20 and 21 –

(a) the provision of services includes the provision of any goods or facilities;
(b) a person is "a provider of services" if he is concerned with the provision, in the United Kingdom, of services to the public or to a section of the public; and
(c) it is irrelevant whether a service is provided on payment or without payment.

(3) The following are examples of services to which this section and sections 20 and 21 apply –

(a) access to and use of any place which members of the public are permitted to enter;
(b) access to and use of means of communication;
(c) access to and use of information services;
(d) accommodation in a hotel, boarding house or other similar establishment;
(e) facilities by way of banking or insurance or for grants, loans, credit or finance;
(f) facilities for entertainment, recreation or refreshment;
(g) facilities provided by employment agencies or under section 2 of the [1973 c. 50.] Employment and Training Act 1973;

(h) the services of any profession or trade, or any local or other public authority.

(4) In the case of an act which constitutes discrimination by virtue of section 55, this section also applies to discrimination against a person who is not disabled.

(5) Except in such circumstances as may be prescribed, this section and sections 20 and 21 do not apply to –
(a) education which is funded, or secured, by a relevant body or provided at –
(i) an establishment which is funded by such a body or by a Minister of the Crown; or
(ii) any other establishment which is a school as defined in section 14(5) of the [1992 c. 13.] Further and Higher Education Act 1992 or section 135(1) of the [1980 c. 44.] Education (Scotland) Act 1980;
(b) any service so far as it consists of the use of any means of transport; or
(c) such other services as may be prescribed.

(6) In subsection (5) "relevant body" means –
(a) a local education authority in England and Wales;
(b) an education authority in Scotland;
(c) the Funding Agency for Schools;
(d) the Schools Funding Council for Wales;
(e) the Further Education Funding Council for England;
(f) the Further Education Funding Council for Wales;
(g) the Higher Education Funding Council for England;
(h) the Scottish Higher Education Funding Council;
(i) the Higher Education Funding Council for Wales;
(j) the Teacher Training Agency;
(k) a voluntary organisation; or
(l) a body of a prescribed kind.

Meaning of "discrimination"

20. (1) For the purposes of section 19, a provider of services discriminates against a disabled person if –
(a) for a reason which relates to the disabled person's disability, he treats him less favourably than he treats or would treat others to whom that reason does not or would not apply; and
(b) he cannot show that the treatment in question is justified.

(2) For the purposes of section 19, a provider of services also discriminates against a disabled person if –
(a) he fails to comply with a section 21 duty imposed on him in relation to the disabled person; and
(b) he cannot show that his failure to comply with that duty is justified.

(3) For the purposes of this section, treatment is justified only if –
(a) in the opinion of the provider of services, one or more of the conditions mentioned in subsection (4) are satisfied; and
(b) it is reasonable, in all the circumstances of the case, for him to hold that opinion.

(4) The conditions are that –
(a) in any case, the treatment is necessary in order not to endanger the health or safety of any person (which may include that of the disabled person);

(b) in any case, the disabled person is incapable of entering into an enforceable agreement, or of giving an informed consent, and for that reason the treatment is reasonable in that case;
(c) in a case falling within section 19(1)(a), the treatment is necessary because the provider of services would otherwise be unable to provide the service to members of the public;
(d) in a case falling within section 19(1)(c) or (d), the treatment is necessary in order for the provider of services to be able to provide the service to the disabled person or to other members of the public;
(e) in a case falling within section 19(1)(d), the difference in the terms on which the service is provided to the disabled person and those on which it is provided to other members of the public reflects the greater cost to the provider of services in providing the service to the disabled person.

(5) Any increase in the cost of providing a service to a disabled person which results from compliance by a provider of services with a section 21 duty shall be disregarded for the purposes of subsection (4)(e).

(6) Regulations may make provision, for purposes of this section, as to circumstances in which –
(a) it is reasonable for a provider of services to hold the opinion mentioned in subsection (3)(a);
(b) it is not reasonable for a provider of services to hold that opinion.

(7) Regulations may make provision for subsection (4)(b) not to apply in prescribed circumstances where –
(a) a person is acting for a disabled person under a power of attorney;
(b) functions conferred by or under Part VII of the [1983 c. 20.] Mental Health Act 1983 are exercisable in relation to a disabled person's property or affairs; or
(c) powers are exercisable in Scotland in relation to a disabled person's property or affairs in consequence of the appointment of a curator bonis, tutor or judicial factor.

(8) Regulations may make provision, for purposes of this section, as to circumstances (other than those mentioned in subsection (4)) in which treatment is to be taken to be justified.

(9) In subsections (3), (4) and (8) "treatment" includes failure to comply with a section 21 duty.

Duty of providers of services to make adjustments

21. (1) Where a provider of services has a practice, policy or procedure which makes it impossible or unreasonably difficult for disabled persons to make use of a service which he provides, or is prepared to provide, to other members of the public, it is his duty to take such steps as it is reasonable, in all the circumstances of the case, for him to have to take in order to change that practice, policy or procedure so that it no longer has that effect.

(2) Where a physical feature (for example, one arising from the design or construction of a building or the approach or access to premises) makes it impossible or unreasonably difficult for disabled persons to make use of such a service, it is the duty of the provider of that service to take such steps as it is reasonable, in all the circumstances of the case, for him to have to take in order to –
(a) remove the feature;

(b) alter it so that it no longer has that effect;
(c) provide a reasonable means of avoiding the feature; or
(d) provide a reasonable alternative method of making the service in question available to disabled persons.

(3) Regulations may prescribe –
(a) matters which are to be taken into account in determining whether any provision of a kind mentioned in subsection (2)(c) or (d) is reasonable; and
(b) categories of providers of services to whom subsection (2) does not apply.

(4) Where an auxiliary aid or service (for example, the provision of information on audio tape or of a sign language interpreter) would –
(a) enable disabled persons to make use of a service which a provider of services provides, or is prepared to provide, to members of the public, or
(b) facilitate the use by disabled persons of such a service, it is the duty of the provider of that service to take such steps as it is reasonable, in all the circumstances of the case, for him to have to take in order to provide that auxiliary aid or service.

(5) Regulations may make provision, for the purposes of this section –
(a) as to circumstances in which it is reasonable for a provider of services to have to take steps of a prescribed description;
(b) as to circumstances in which it is not reasonable for a provider of services to have to take steps of a prescribed description;
(c) as to what is to be included within the meaning of "practice, policy or procedure"
(d) as to what is not to be included within the meaning of that expression;
(e) as to things which are to be treated as physical features;
(f) as to things which are not to be treated as such features;
(g) as to things which are to be treated as auxiliary aids or services;
(h) as to things which are not to be treated as auxiliary aids or services.

(6) Nothing in this section requires a provider of services to take any steps which would fundamentally alter the nature of the service in question or the nature of his trade, profession or business.

(7) Nothing in this section requires a provider of services to take any steps which would cause him to incur expenditure exceeding the prescribed maximum.

(8) Regulations under subsection (7) may provide for the prescribed maximum to be calculated by reference to –
(a) aggregate amounts of expenditure incurred in relation to different cases;
(b) prescribed periods;
(c) services of a prescribed description;
(d) premises of a prescribed description; or
(e) such other criteria as may be prescribed.

(9) Regulations may provide, for the purposes of subsection (7), for expenditure incurred by one provider of services to be treated as incurred by another.

(10) This section imposes duties only for the purpose of determining whether a provider of services has discriminated against a disabled person; and accordingly a breach of any such duty is not actionable as such.

Premises

Discrimination in relation to premises

22. (1) It is unlawful for a person with power to dispose of any premises to discriminate against a disabled person –

(a) in the terms on which he offers to dispose of those premises to the disabled person;

(b) by refusing to dispose of those premises to the disabled person; or

(c) in his treatment of the disabled person in relation to any list of persons in need of premises of that description.

(2) Subsection (1) does not apply to a person who owns an estate or interest in the premises and wholly occupies them unless, for the purpose of disposing of the premises, he –

(a) uses the services of an estate agent, or

(b) publishes an advertisement or causes an advertisement to be published.

(3) It is unlawful for a person managing any premises to discriminate against a disabled person occupying those premises –

(a) in the way he permits the disabled person to make use of any benefits or facilities;

(b) by refusing or deliberately omitting to permit the disabled person to make use of any benefits or facilities; or

(c) by evicting the disabled person, or subjecting him to any other detriment.

(4) It is unlawful for any person whose licence or consent is required for the disposal of any premises comprised in, or (in Scotland) the subject of, a tenancy to discriminate against a disabled person by withholding his licence or consent for the disposal of the premises to the disabled person.

(5) Subsection (4) applies to tenancies created before as well as after the passing of this Act.

(6) In this section –

"advertisement" includes every form of advertisement or notice, whether to the public or not;

"dispose", in relation to premises, includes granting a right to occupy the premises, and, in relation to premises comprised in, or (in Scotland) the subject of, a tenancy, includes –

(a) assigning the tenancy, and

(b) sub-letting or parting with possession of the premises or any part of the premises;

and "disposal" shall be construed accordingly;

"estate agent" means a person who, by way of profession or trade, provides services for the purpose of finding premises for persons seeking to acquire them or assisting in the disposal of premises; and

"tenancy" means a tenancy created –

(a) by a lease or sub-lease,

(b) by an agreement for a lease or sub-lease,

(c) by a tenancy agreement, or

(d) in pursuance of any enactment.

(7) In the case of an act which constitutes discrimination by virtue of section 55, this section also applies to discrimination against a person who is not disabled.

(8) This section applies only in relation to premises in the United Kingdom.

Exemption for small dwellings

23. (1) Where the conditions mentioned in subsection (2) are satisfied, subsection (1), (3) or (as the case may be) (4) of section 22 does not apply.

(2) The conditions are that –

(a) the relevant occupier resides, and intends to continue to reside, on the premises;

(b) the relevant occupier shares accommodation on the premises with persons who reside on the premises and are not members of his household;

(c) the shared accommodation is not storage accommodation or a means of access; and

(d) the premises are small premises.

(3) For the purposes of this section, premises are "small premises" if they fall within subsection (4) or (5).

(4) Premises fall within this subsection if –

(a) only the relevant occupier and members of his household reside in the accommodation occupied by him;

(b) the premises comprise, in addition to the accommodation occupied by the relevant occupier, residential accommodation for at least one other household;

(c) the residential accommodation for each other household is let, or available for letting, on a separate tenancy or similar agreement; and

(d) there are not normally more than two such other households.

(5) Premises fall within this subsection if there is not normally residential accommodation on the premises for more than six persons in addition to the relevant occupier and any members of his household.

(6) For the purposes of this section "the relevant occupier" means –

(a) in a case falling within section 22(1), the person with power to dispose of the premises, or a near relative of his;

(b) in a case falling within section 22(4), the person whose licence or consent is required for the disposal of the premises, or a near relative of his.

(7) For the purposes of this section –

"near relative" means a person's spouse, partner, parent, child, grandparent, grandchild, or brother or sister (whether of full or half blood or by affinity); and

"partner" means the other member of a couple consisting of a man and a woman who are not married to each other but are living together as husband and wife.

Meaning of "discrimination"

24. (1) For the purposes of section 22, a person ("A") discriminates against a disabled person if –

(a) for a reason which relates to the disabled person's disability, he treats him less favourably than he treats or would treat others to whom that reason does not or would not apply; and

(b) he cannot show that the treatment in question is justified.

(2) For the purposes of this section, treatment is justified only if –

(a) in A's opinion, one or more of the conditions mentioned in subsection (3) are satisfied; and
(b) it is reasonable, in all the circumstances of the case, for him to hold that opinion.

(3) The conditions are that –
(a) in any case, the treatment is necessary in order not to endanger the health or safety of any person (which may include that of the disabled person);
(b) in any case, the disabled person is incapable of entering into an enforceable agreement, or of giving an informed consent, and for that reason the treatment is reasonable in that case;
(c) in a case falling within section 22(3)(a), the treatment is necessary in order for the disabled person or the occupiers of other premises forming part of the building to make use of the benefit or facility;
(d) in a case falling within section 22(3)(b), the treatment is necessary in order for the occupiers of other premises forming part of the building to make use of the benefit or facility.

(4) Regulations may make provision, for purposes of this section, as to circumstances in which –
(a) it is reasonable for a person to hold the opinion mentioned in subsection 2(a);
(b) it is not reasonable for a person to hold that opinion.

(5) Regulations may make provision, for purposes of this section, as to circumstances (other than those mentioned in subsection (3)) in which treatment is to be taken to be justified.

Enforcement, etc.

Enforcement, remedies and procedure

25. (1) A claim by any person that another person –
(a) has discriminated against him in a way which is unlawful under this Part; or
(b) is by virtue of section 57 or 58 to be treated as having discriminated against him in such a way, may be made the subject of civil proceedings in the same way as any other claim in tort or (in Scotland) in reparation for breach of statutory duty.

(2) For the avoidance of doubt it is hereby declared that damages in respect of discrimination in a way which is unlawful under this Part may include compensation for injury to feelings whether or not they include compensation under any other head.

(3) Proceedings in England and Wales shall be brought only in a county court.

(4) Proceedings in Scotland shall be brought only in a sheriff court.

(5) The remedies available in such proceedings are those which are available in the High Court or (as the case may be) the Court of Session.

(6) Part II of Schedule 3 makes further provision about the enforcement of this Part and about procedure.

Validity and revision of certain agreements

26. (1) Any term in a contract for the provision of goods, facilities or services or in any other agreement is void so far as it purports to –

(a) require a person to do anything which would contravene any provision of, or made under, this Part,
(b) exclude or limit the operation of any provision of this Part, or
(c) prevent any person from making a claim under this Part.

(2) Paragraphs (b) and (c) of subsection (1) do not apply to an agreement settling a claim to which section 25 applies.

(3) On the application of any person interested in an agreement to which subsection (1) applies, a county court or a sheriff court may make such order as it thinks just for modifying the agreement to take account of the effect of subsection (1).

(4) No such order shall be made unless all persons affected have been –
(a) given notice of the application; and
(b) afforded an opportunity to make representations to the court.

(5) Subsection (4) applies subject to any rules of court providing for that notice to be dispensed with.

(6) An order under subsection (3) may include provision as respects any period before the making of the order.

Alterations to premises occupied under leases

27. (1) This section applies where –
(a) a provider of services ("the occupier") occupies premises under a lease;
(b) but for this section, he would not be entitled to make a particular alteration to the premises; and
(c) the alteration is one which the occupier proposes to make in order to comply with a section 21 duty.

(2) Except to the extent to which it expressly so provides, the lease shall have effect by virtue of this subsection as if it provided –
(a) for the occupier to be entitled to make the alteration with the written consent of the lessor;
(b) for the occupier to have to make a written application to the lessor for consent if he wishes to make the alteration;
(c) if such an application is made, for the lessor not to withhold his consent unreasonably; and
(d) for the lessor to be entitled to make his consent subject to reasonable conditions.

(3) In this section –
"lease" includes a tenancy, sub-lease or sub-tenancy and an agreement for a lease, tenancy, sub-lease or sub-tenancy; and
"sub-lease" and "sub-tenancy" have such meaning as may be prescribed.

(4) If the terms and conditions of a lease –
(a) impose conditions which are to apply if the occupier alters the premises, or
(b) entitle the lessor to impose conditions when consenting to the occupier's altering the premises

the occupier is to be treated for the purposes of subsection (1) as not being entitled to make the alteration.

(5) Part II of Schedule 4 supplements the provisions of this section.

Advice and assistance

28. (1) The Secretary of State may make arrangements for the provision of advice and assistance to persons with a view to promoting the settlement of disputes arising under this Part otherwise than by recourse to the courts.

(2) Any person appointed by the Secretary of State in connection with arrangements made under subsection (1) shall have such duties as the Secretary of State may direct.

(3) The Secretary of State may pay to any person so appointed such allowances and compensation for loss of earnings as he considers appropriate.

(4) The Secretary of State may make such payments, by way of grants, in respect of expenditure incurred, or to be incurred, by any person exercising functions in accordance with arrangements made by the Secretary of State under this section as he considers appropriate.

(5) The approval of the Treasury is required for any payment under subsection (3) or (4).

PART IV

Education

Education of disabled persons

29. (1) In section 161(5) of the [1993 c. 62.] Education Act 1993 (information relating to pupils with special educational needs to be included in annual report), omit the words from "and in this subsection" to the end.

(2) After section 161(5) of that Act insert –

"(6) The annual report for each county, voluntary or grant-maintained school shall include a report containing information as to –

(a) the arrangements for the admission of disabled pupils;

(b) the steps taken to prevent disabled pupils from being treated less favourably than other pupils; and

(c) the facilities provided to assist access to the school by disabled pupils.

(7) In this section –

"annual report" means the report prepared under the articles of government for the school in accordance with section 30 of the [1986 c. 61.] Education (No. 2) Act 1986 or, as the case may be, paragraph 8 of Schedule 6 to this Act; and "disabled pupils" means pupils who are disabled persons for the purposes of the [1995 c. 50.] Disability Discrimination Act 1995."

(3) In section 1 of the [1994 c. 30.] Education Act 1994 (establishment of the Teacher Training Agency) add, at the end –

"(4) In exercising their functions, the Teacher Training Agency shall have regard to the requirements of persons who are disabled persons for the purposes of the Disability Discrimination Act 1995."

Further and higher education of disabled persons – 1992 c. 13

30. (1) The Further and Higher Education Act 1992 is amended as set out in subsections (2) to (6).

(2) In section 5 (administration of funds by further education funding councils), in subsection (6)(b), after "may" insert ", subject to subsection (7A) below,".

(3) After section 5(7) insert –

"(7A) Without prejudice to the power to impose conditions given by subsection (6)(b) above, the conditions subject to which a council gives financial support under this section to the governing body of an institution within the further education sector –

(a) shall require the governing body to publish disability statements at such intervals as may be prescribed; and

(b) may include conditions relating to the provision made, or to be made, by the institution with respect to disabled persons.

(7B) For the purposes of subsection (7A) above –

"disability statement" means a statement containing information of a prescribed description about the provision of facilities for education made by the institution in respect of disabled persons;

"disabled persons" means persons who are disabled persons for the purposes of the [1995 c. 50.] Disability Discrimination Act 1995; and

"prescribed" means prescribed by regulations"

(4) In section 8 (supplementary functions) add, at the end –

"(6) As soon as is reasonably practicable after the end of its financial year, each council shall make a written report to the Secretary of State on –

(a) the progress made during the year to which the report relates in the provision of further education for disabled students in their area; and

(b) their plans for the future provision of further education for disabled students in their area.

(7) In subsection (6) above –

"disabled students" means students who are disabled persons for the purposes of the Disability Discrimination Act 1995; and

"financial year" means the period of twelve months ending with 31st March 1997 and each successive period of twelve months."

(5) In section 62 (establishment of higher education funding councils), after subsection (7) insert –

"(7A) In exercising their functions, each council shall have regard to the requirements of disabled persons.

(7B) In subsection (7A) "disabled persons" means persons who are disabled persons for the purposes of the Disability Discrimination Act 1995."

(6) In section 65 (administration of funds by higher education funding councils), after subsection (4) insert –

"(4A) Without prejudice to the power to impose conditions given by subsection (3) above, the conditions subject to which a council makes grants, loans or other payments under this section to the governing body of a higher education institution shall require the governing body to publish disability statements at such intervals as may be specified.

(4B) For the purposes of subsection (4A) above –

"disability statement" means a statement containing information of a specified description about the provision of facilities for education and research made by the institution in respect of persons who are disabled persons for the purposes of the Disability Discrimination Act 1995; and

"specified" means specified in the conditions subject to which grants, loans or other payments are made by a council under this section."

(7) The Education Act 1944 is amended as set out in subsections (8) and (9).

(8) In section 41 (functions of local education authorities in respect of further education), after subsection (2) insert –

"(2A) It shall be the duty of every local education authority to publish disability statements at such intervals as may be prescribed.

(2B) For the purposes of subsection (2A) above –

"disability statement" means a statement containing information of a prescribed description about the provision of facilities for further education made by the local education authority in respect of persons who are disabled persons for the purposes of the [1995 c. 50.] Disability Discrimination Act 1995; and

"prescribed" means prescribed by regulations made by the Secretary of State."

(9) In section 41(7), (8) and (11), for "this section" substitute "subsections (1) and (6) above".

Further and higher education of disabled persons: Scotland –1992 c. 37

31. (1) The Further and Higher Education (Scotland) Act 1992 is amended as follows.

(2) In section 37 (establishment of Scottish Higher Education Funding Council) after subsection (4) insert –

"(4A) In exercising their functions, the Council shall have regard to the requirements of disabled persons.

(4B) In subsection (4A) above, "disabled persons" means persons who are disabled persons for the purpose of the Disability Discrimination Act 1995."

(3) In section 40 (administration of funds by the Council), after subsection (4) insert –

"(5) Without prejudice to the power to impose conditions given by subsection (3) above, the conditions subject to which the Council make grants, loans or other payments under this section to the governing body of an institution within the higher education sector shall require the governing body to publish disability statements at such intervals as may be specified.

(6) For the purposes of subsection (5) above –

"disability statement" means a statement containing information of a specified description about the provision of facilities for education and research made by the institution in respect of persons who are disabled persons for the purpose of the Disability Discrimination Act 1995; and

"specified" means specified in the conditions subject to which grants, loans or other payments are made by the Council under this section."

PART V
Public Transport
Taxis

Taxi accessibility regulations

32. (1) The Secretary of State may make regulations ("taxi accessibility regulations") for the purpose of securing that it is possible –

(a) for disabled persons –

(i) to get into and out of taxis in safety;

(ii) to be carried in taxis in safety and in reasonable comfort; and

(b) for disabled persons in wheelchairs –
(i)to be conveyed in safety into and out of taxis while remaining in their wheelchairs; and
(ii) to be carried in taxis in safety and in reasonable comfort while remaining in their wheelchairs.

(2) Taxi accessibility regulations may, in particular –
(a) require any regulated taxi to conform with provisions of the regulations as to –
(i) the size of any door opening which is for the use of passengers;
(ii) the floor area of the passenger compartment;
(iii) the amount of headroom in the passenger compartment;
(iv) the fitting of restraining devices designed to ensure the stability of a wheelchair while the taxi is moving;
(b) require the driver of any regulated taxi which is plying for hire, or which has been hired, to comply with provisions of the regulations as to the carrying of ramps or other devices designed to facilitate the loading and unloading of wheelchairs;
(c) require the driver of any regulated taxi in which a disabled person who is in a wheelchair is being carried (while remaining in his wheelchair) to comply with provisions of the regulations as to the position in which the wheelchair is to be secured.

(3) The driver of a regulated taxi which is plying for hire, or which has been hired, is guilty of an offence if –
(a) he fails to comply with any requirement imposed on him by the regulations; or
(b) the taxi fails to conform with any provision of the regulations with which it is required to conform.

(4) A person who is guilty of such an offence is liable, on summary conviction, to a fine not exceeding level 3 on the standard scale.

(5) In this section –
"passenger compartment" has such meaning as may be prescribed;
"regulated taxi" means any taxi to which the regulations are expressed to apply;
"taxi" means a vehicle licensed under –
(a) section 37 of the [1847 c. 89.] Town Police Clauses Act 1847, or
(b) section 6 of the [1869 c. 115.] Metropolitan Public Carriage Act 1869,
but does not include a taxi which is drawn by a horse or other animal.

Designated transport facilities

33. (1) In this section "a franchise agreement" means a contract entered into by the operator of a designated transport facility for the provision by the other party to the contract of hire car services –
(a) for members of the public using any part of the transport facility; and
(b) which involve vehicles entering any part of that facility.

(2) The Secretary of State may by regulations provide for the application of any taxi provision in relation to –
(a) vehicles used for the provision of services under a franchise agreement; or
(b) the drivers of such vehicles.

(3) Any regulations under subsection (2) may apply any taxi provision with such modifications as the Secretary of State considers appropriate.

(4) In this section –

"designated" means designated for the purposes of this section by an order made by the Secretary of State;

"hire car" has such meaning as may be prescribed;

"operator", in relation to a transport facility, means any person who is concerned with the management or operation of the facility;

"taxi provision" means any provision of –

(a) this Act, or

(b) regulations made in pursuance of section 20(2A) of the [1982 c. 45.] Civic Government (Scotland) Act 1982, which applies in relation to taxis or the drivers of taxis; and

"transport facility" means any premises which form part of any port, airport, railway station or bus station.

New licences conditional on compliance with taxi accessibility regulations

34. (1) No licensing authority shall grant a licence for a taxi to ply for hire unless the vehicle conforms with those provisions of the taxi accessibility regulations with which it will be required to conform if licensed.

(2) Subsection (1) does not apply if such a licence was in force with respect to the vehicle at any time during the period of 28 days immediately before the day on which the licence is granted.

(3) The Secretary of State may by order provide for subsection (2) to cease to have effect on such date as may be specified in the order.

(4) Separate orders may be made under subsection (3) with respect to different areas or localities.

Exemption from taxi accessibility regulations

35. (1) The Secretary of State may make regulations ("exemption regulations") for the purpose of enabling any relevant licensing authority to apply to him for an order (an "exemption order") exempting the authority from the requirements of section 34.

(2) Exemption regulations may, in particular, make provision requiring a licensing authority proposing to apply for an exemption order –

(a) to carry out such consultations as may be prescribed;

(b) to publish the proposal in the prescribed manner;

(c) to consider any representations made to it about the proposal, before applying for the order;

(d) to make its application in the prescribed form.

(3) A licensing authority may apply for an exemption order only if it is satisfied –

(a) that, having regard to the circumstances prevailing in its area, it would be inappropriate for the requirements of section 34 to apply; and

(b) that the application of section 34 would result in an unacceptable reduction in the number of taxis in its area.

(4) After considering any application for an exemption order and consulting the Disabled Persons Transport Advisory Committee and such other persons as he considers appropriate, the Secretary of State may –

(a) make an exemption order in the terms of the application;

(b) make an exemption order in such other terms as he considers appropriate; or

(c) refuse to make an exemption order.

(5) The Secretary of State may by regulations ("swivel seat regulations") make provision requiring any exempt taxi plying for hire in an area in respect of which an exemption order is in force to conform with provisions of the regulations as to the fitting and use of swivel seats.

(6) The Secretary of State may by regulations make provision with respect to swivel seat regulations similar to that made by section 34 with respect to taxi accessibility regulations.

(7) In this section –

"exempt taxi" means a taxi in relation to which section 34(1) would apply if the exemption order were not in force;

"relevant licensing authority" means a licensing authority responsible for licensing taxis in any area of England and Wales other than the area to which the [1869 c. 115.] Metropolitan Public Carriage Act 1869 applies; and

"swivel seats" has such meaning as may be prescribed.

Carrying of passengers in wheelchairs

36. (1) This section imposes duties on the driver of a regulated taxi which has been hired –

(a) by or for a disabled person who is in a wheelchair; or

(b) by a person who wishes such a disabled person to accompany him in the taxi.

(2) In this section –

"carry" means carry in the taxi concerned; and

"the passenger" means the disabled person concerned.

(3) The duties are –

(a) to carry the passenger while he remains in his wheelchair;

(b) not to make any additional charge for doing so;

(c) if the passenger chooses to sit in a passenger seat, to carry the wheelchair;

(d) to take such steps as are necessary to ensure that the passenger is carried in safety and in reasonable comfort;

(e) to give such assistance as may be reasonably required –

(i) to enable the passenger to get into or out of the taxi;

(ii) if the passenger wishes to remain in his wheelchair, to enable him to be conveyed into and out of the taxi while in his wheelchair;

(iii) to load the passenger's luggage into or out of the taxi;

(iv) if the passenger does not wish to remain in his wheelchair, to load the wheelchair into or out of the taxi.

(4) Nothing in this section is to be taken to require the driver of any taxi –

(a) except in the case of a taxi of a prescribed description, to carry more than one person in a wheelchair, or more than one wheelchair, on any one journey; or

(b) to carry any person in circumstances in which it would otherwise be lawful for him to refuse to carry that person.

(5) A driver of a regulated taxi who fails to comply with any duty imposed on him by this section is guilty of an offence and liable, on summary conviction, to a fine not exceeding level 3 on the standard scale.

(6) In any proceedings for an offence under this section, it is a defence for the accused to show that, even though at the time of the alleged offence the taxi conformed with those provisions of the taxi accessibility regulations with which it was required to conform, it would not have been possible for the wheelchair in question to be carried in safety in the taxi.

(7) If the licensing authority is satisfied that it is appropriate to exempt a person from the duties imposed by this section –
(a) on medical grounds, or
(b) on the ground that his physical condition makes it impossible or unreasonably difficult for him to comply with the duties imposed on drivers by this section,
it shall issue him with a certificate of exemption.

(8) A certificate of exemption shall be issued for such period as may be specified in the certificate.

(9) The driver of a regulated taxi is exempt from the duties imposed by this section if –
(a) a certificate of exemption issued to him under this section is in force; and
(b) the prescribed notice of his exemption is exhibited on the taxi in the prescribed manner.

Carrying of guide dogs and hearing dogs

37. (1) This section imposes duties on the driver of a taxi which has been hired –
(a) by or for a disabled person who is accompanied by his guide dog or hearing dog, or
(b) by a person who wishes such a disabled person to accompany him in the taxi.

(2) The disabled person is referred to in this section as "the passenger" .

(3) The duties are –
(a) to carry the passenger's dog and allow it to remain with the passenger; and
(b) not to make any additional charge for doing so.

(4) A driver of a taxi who fails to comply with any duty imposed on him by this section is guilty of an offence and liable, on summary conviction, to a fine not exceeding level 3 on the standard scale.

(5) If the licensing authority is satisfied that it is appropriate on medical grounds to exempt a person from the duties imposed by this section, it shall issue him with a certificate of exemption.

(6) In determining whether to issue a certificate of exemption, the licensing authority shall, in particular, have regard to the physical characteristics of the taxi which the applicant drives or those of any kind of taxi in relation to which he requires the certificate.

(7) A certificate of exemption shall be issued –
(a) with respect to a specified taxi or a specified kind of taxi; and
(b) for such period as may be specified in the certificate.

(8) The driver of a taxi is exempt from the duties imposed by this section if –
(a) a certificate of exemption issued to him under this section is in force with respect to the taxi; and

(b) the prescribed notice of his exemption is exhibited on the taxi in the prescribed manner.

(9) The Secretary of State may, for the purposes of this section, prescribe any other category of dog trained to assist a disabled person who has a disability of a prescribed kind.

(10) This section applies in relation to any such prescribed category of dog as it applies in relation to guide dogs.

(11) In this section –

"guide dog" means a dog which has been trained to guide a blind person; and

"hearing dog" means a dog which has been trained to assist a deaf person.

Appeal against refusal of exemption certificate

38. (1) Any person who is aggrieved by the refusal of a licensing authority to issue an exemption certificate under section 36 or 37 may appeal to the appropriate court before the end of the period of 28 days beginning with the date of the refusal.

(2) On an appeal to it under this section, the court may direct the licensing authority concerned to issue the appropriate certificate of exemption to have effect for such period as may be specified in the direction.

(3) "Appropriate court" means the magistrates' court for the petty sessions area in which the licensing authority has its principal office.

Requirements as to disabled passengers in Scotland

39. (1) Part II of the [1982 c. 45.] Civic Government (Scotland) Act 1982 (licensing and regulation) is amended as follows.

(2) In subsection (4) of section 10 (suitability of vehicle for use as taxi) –

(a) after "authority" insert

" – (a)" and

(b) at the end add

"and

(b) as not being so suitable if it does not so comply."

(3) In section 20 (regulations relating to taxis etc.) after subsection (2) insert –

"(2A) Without prejudice to the generality of subsections (1) and (2) above, regulations under those subsections may make such provision as appears to the Secretary of State to be necessary or expedient in relation to the carrying in taxis of disabled persons (within the meaning of section 1(2) of the [1995 c. 50.] Disability Discrimination Act 1995) and such provision may in particular prescribe –

(a) requirements as to the carriage of wheelchairs, guide dogs, hearing dogs and other categories of dog;

(b) a date from which any such provision is to apply and the extent to which it is to apply; and

(c) the circumstances in which an exemption from such provision may be granted in respect of any taxi or taxi driver,

and in this subsection –

"guide dog" means a dog which has been trained to guide a blind person;

"hearing dog" means a dog which has been trained to assist a deaf person; and "other categories of dog" means such other categories of dog as the Secretary of State may prescribe, trained to assist disabled persons who have disabilities of such kinds as he may prescribe."

Public service vehicles

PSV accessibility regulations

40. (1) The Secretary of State may make regulations ("PSV accessibility regulations") for the purpose of securing that it is possible for disabled persons –

(a) to get on to and off regulated public service vehicles in safety and without unreasonable difficulty (and, in the case of disabled persons in wheelchairs, to do so while remaining in their wheelchairs); and

(b) to be carried in such vehicles in safety and in reasonable comfort.

(2) PSV accessibility regulations may, in particular, make provision as to the construction, use and maintenance of regulated public service vehicles including provision as to –

(a) the fitting of equipment to vehicles;

(b) equipment to be carried by vehicles;

(c) the design of equipment to be fitted to, or carried by, vehicles;

(d) the fitting and use of restraining devices designed to ensure the stability of wheelchairs while vehicles are moving;

(e) the position in which wheelchairs are to be secured while vehicles are moving.

(3) Any person who –

(a) contravenes or fails to comply with any provision of the PSV accessibility regulations,

(b) uses on a road a regulated public service vehicle which does not conform with any provision of the regulations with which it is required to conform, or

(c) causes or permits to be used on a road such a regulated public service vehicle,

is guilty of an offence.

(4) A person who is guilty of such an offence is liable, on summary conviction, to a fine not exceeding level 4 on the standard scale.

(5) In this section –

"public service vehicle" means a vehicle which is –

(a) adapted to carry more than eight passengers; and

(b) a public service vehicle for the purposes of the [1981 c. 14.] Public Passenger Vehicles Act 1981;

"regulated public service vehicle" means any public service vehicle to which the PSV accessibility regulations are expressed to apply.

(6) Different provision may be made in regulations under this section –

(a) as respects different classes or descriptions of vehicle;

(b) as respects the same class or description of vehicle in different circumstances.

(7) Before making any regulations under this section or section 41 or 42 the Secretary of State shall consult the Disabled Persons Transport Advisory Committee and such other representative organisations as he thinks fit.

Accessibility certificates

41. (1) A regulated public service vehicle shall not be used on a road unless –

(a) a vehicle examiner has issued a certificate (an "accessibility certificate") that such provisions of the PSV accessibility regulations as may be prescribed are satisfied in respect of the vehicle; or

(b) an approval certificate has been issued under section 42 in respect of the vehicle.

(2) The Secretary of State may make regulations –

(a) with respect to applications for, and the issue of, accessibility certificates;

(b) providing for the examination of vehicles in respect of which applications have been made;

(c) with respect to the issue of copies of accessibility certificates in place of certificates which have been lost or destroyed.

(3) If a regulated public service vehicle is used in contravention of this section, the operator of the vehicle is guilty of an offence and liable on summary conviction to a fine not exceeding level 4 on the standard scale.

(4) In this section "operator" has the same meaning as in the [1981 c. 14.] Public Passenger Vehicles Act 1981.

Approval certificates

42. (1) Where the Secretary of State is satisfied that such provisions of the PSV accessibility regulations as may be prescribed for the purposes of section 41 are satisfied in respect of a particular vehicle he may approve the vehicle for the purposes of this section.

(2) A vehicle which has been so approved is referred to in this section as a "type vehicle".

(3) Subsection (4) applies where a declaration in the prescribed form has been made by an authorised person that a particular vehicle conforms in design, construction and equipment with a type vehicle.

(4) A vehicle examiner may, after examining (if he thinks fit) the vehicle to which the declaration applies, issue a certificate in the prescribed form ("an approval certificate") that it conforms to the type vehicle.

(5) The Secretary of State may make regulations –

(a) with respect to applications for, and grants of, approval under subsection (1);

(b) with respect to applications for, and the issue of, approval certificates;

(c) providing for the examination of vehicles in respect of which applications have been made;

(d) with respect to the issue of copies of approval certificates in place of certificates which have been lost or destroyed.

(6) The Secretary of State may at any time withdraw his approval of a type vehicle.

(7) Where an approval is withdrawn –

(a) no further approval certificates shall be issued by reference to the type vehicle; but

(b) any approval certificate issued by reference to the type vehicle before the withdrawal shall continue to have effect for the purposes of section 41.

(8) In subsection (3) "authorised person" means a person authorised by the Secretary of State for the purposes of that subsection.

Special authorisations

43. (1) The Secretary of State may by order authorise the use on roads of –

(a) any regulated public service vehicle of a class or description specified by the order, or

(b) any regulated public service vehicle which is so specified,

and nothing in section 40, 41 or 42 prevents the use of any vehicle in accordance with the order.

(2) Any such authorisation may be given subject to such restrictions and conditions as may be specified by or under the order.

(3) The Secretary of State may by order make provision for the purpose of securing that, subject to such restrictions and conditions as may be specified by or under the order, provisions of the PSV accessibility regulations apply to regulated public service vehicles of a description specified by the order subject to such modifications or exceptions as may be specified by the order.

Reviews and appeals

44. (1) Subsection (2) applies where –

(a) the Secretary of State refuses an application for the approval of a vehicle under section 42(1); and

(b) before the end of the prescribed period, the applicant asks the Secretary of State to review the decision and pays any fee fixed under section 45.

(2) The Secretary of State shall –

(a) review the decision; and

(b) in doing so, consider any representations made to him in writing, before the end of the prescribed period, by the applicant.

(3) A person applying for an accessibility certificate or an approval certificate may appeal to the Secretary of State against the refusal of a vehicle examiner to issue such a certificate.

(4) An appeal must be made within the prescribed time and in the prescribed manner.

(5) Regulations may make provision as to the procedure to be followed in connection with appeals.

(6) On the determination of an appeal, the Secretary of State may –

(a) confirm, vary or reverse the decision appealed against;

(b) give such directions as he thinks fit to the vehicle examiner for giving effect to his decision.

Fees

45. (1) Such fees, payable at such times, as may be prescribed may be charged by the Secretary of State in respect of –

(a) applications for, and grants of, approval under section 42(1);

(b) applications for, and the issue of, accessibility certificates and approval certificates;

(c) copies of such certificates;

(d) reviews and appeals under section 44.

(2) Any such fees received by the Secretary of State shall be paid by him into the Consolidated Fund.

(3) Regulations under subsection (1) may make provision for the repayment of fees, in whole or in part, in such circumstances as may be prescribed.

(4) Before making any regulations under subsection (1) the Secretary of State shall consult such representative organisations as he thinks fit.

Rail vehicles

Rail vehicle accessibility regulations

46. – (1) The Secretary of State may make regulations ("rail vehicle accessibility regulations") for the purpose of securing that it is possible –

(a) for disabled persons –

(i) to get on to and off regulated rail vehicles in safety and without unreasonable difficulty;

(ii) to be carried in such vehicles in safety and in reasonable comfort; and

(b) for disabled persons in wheelchairs –

(i) to get on to and off such vehicles in safety and without unreasonable difficulty while remaining in their wheelchairs, and

(ii) to be carried in such vehicles in safety and in reasonable comfort while remaining in their wheelchairs.

(2) Rail vehicle accessibility regulations may, in particular, make provision as to the construction, use and maintenance of regulated rail vehicles including provision as to –

(a) the fitting of equipment to vehicles;
(b) equipment to be carried by vehicles;
(c) the design of equipment to be fitted to, or carried by, vehicles;
(d) the use of equipment fitted to, or carried by, vehicles;
(e) the toilet facilities to be provided in vehicles;
(f) the location and floor area of the wheelchair accommodation to be provided in vehicles;
(g) assistance to be given to disabled persons.

(3) If a regulated rail vehicle which does not conform with any provision of the rail vehicle accessibility regulations with which it is required to conform is used for carriage, the operator of the vehicle is guilty of an offence.

(4) A person who is guilty of such an offence is liable, on summary conviction, to a fine not exceeding level 4 on the standard scale.

(5) Different provision may be made in rail vehicle accessibility regulations –

(a) as respects different classes or descriptions of rail vehicle;
(b) as respects the same class or description of rail vehicle in different circumstances;
(c) as respects different networks.

(6) In this section –

"network" means any permanent way or other means of guiding or supporting rail vehicles or any section of it;

"operator", in relation to any rail vehicle, means the person having the management of that vehicle;

"rail vehicle" means a vehicle –

(a) constructed or adapted to carry passengers on any railway, tramway or prescribed system; and
(b) first brought into use, or belonging to a class of vehicle first brought into use, after 31st December 1998;

"regulated rail vehicle" means any rail vehicle to which the rail vehicle accessibility regulations are expressed to apply; and
"wheelchair accommodation" has such meaning as may be prescribed.

(7) In subsection (6) –
"prescribed system" means a system using a prescribed mode of guided transport ("guided transport" having the same meaning as in the [1992 c. 42.] Transport and Works Act 1992); and
"railway" and "tramway" have the same meaning as in that Act.

(8) The Secretary of State may by regulations make provision as to the time when a rail vehicle, or a class of rail vehicle, is to be treated, for the purposes of this section, as first brought into use.

(9) Regulations under subsection (8) may include provision for disregarding periods of testing and other prescribed periods of use.

(10) For the purposes of this section and section 47, a person uses a vehicle for carriage if he uses it for the carriage of members of the public for hire or reward at separate fares.

(11) Before making any regulations under subsection (1) or section 47 the Secretary of State shall consult the Disabled Persons Transport Advisory Committee and such other representative organisations as he thinks fit.

Exemption from rail vehicle accessibility regulations

47. (1) The Secretary of State may by order (an "exemption order") authorise the use for carriage of any regulated rail vehicle of a specified description, or in specified circumstances, even though that vehicle does not conform with the provisions of the rail vehicle accessibility regulations with which it is required to conform.

(2) Regulations may make provision with respect to exemption orders including, in particular, provision as to –
(a) the persons by whom applications for exemption orders may be made;
(b) the form in which such applications are to be made;
(c) information to be supplied in connection with such applications;
(d) the period for which exemption orders are to continue in force;
(e) the revocation of exemption orders.

(3) After considering any application for an exemption order and consulting the Disabled Persons Transport Advisory Committee and such other persons as he considers appropriate, the Secretary of State may –
(a) make an exemption order in the terms of the application;
(b) make an exemption order in such other terms as he considers appropriate;
(c) refuse to make an exemption order.

(4) An exemption order may be made subject to such restrictions and conditions as may be specified.

(5) In this section "specified" means specified in an exemption order.

Supplemental

Offences by bodies corporate etc.

48. (1) Where an offence under section 40 or 46 committed by a body corporate is committed with the consent or connivance of, or is attributable to any neglect on the part of, a director, manager, secretary or other similar officer of the body, or a person purporting to act in such a capacity, he as well as the body corporate is guilty of the offence.

(2) In subsection (1) "director" , in relation to a body corporate whose affairs are managed by its members, means a member of the body corporate.

(3) Where, in Scotland, an offence under section 40 or 46 committed by a partnership or by an unincorporated association other than a partnership is committed with the consent or connivance of, or is attributable to any neglect on the part of, a partner in the partnership or (as the case may be) a person concerned in the management or control of the association, he, as well as the partnership or association, is guilty of the offence.

Forgery and false statements

49. (1) In this section "relevant document" means –

(a) a certificate of exemption issued under section 36 or 37;
(b) a notice of a kind mentioned in section 36(9)(b) or 37(8)(b);
(c) an accessibility certificate; or
(d) an approval certificate.

(2) A person is guilty of an offence if, with intent to deceive, he –

(a) forges, alters or uses a relevant document;
(b) lends a relevant document to any other person;
(c) allows a relevant document to be used by any other person; or
(d) makes or has in his possession any document which closely resembles a relevant document.

(3) A person who is guilty of an offence under subsection (2) is liable –

(a) on summary conviction, to a fine not exceeding the statutory maximum;
(b) on conviction on indictment, to imprisonment for a term not exceeding two years or to a fine or to both.

(4) A person who knowingly makes a false statement for the purpose of obtaining an accessibility certificate or an approval certificate is guilty of an offence and liable on summary conviction to a fine not exceeding level 4 on the standard scale.

PART VI

The National Disability Council

The National Disability Council

50. (1) There shall be a body to be known as the National Disability Council (but in this Act referred to as "the Council").

(2) It shall be the duty of the Council to advise the Secretary of State, either on its own initiative or when asked to do so by the Secretary of State –

(a) on matters relevant to the elimination of discrimination against disabled persons and persons who have had a disability;
(b) on measures which are likely to reduce or eliminate such discrimination; and
(c) on matters related to the operation of this Act or of provisions made under this Act.

(3) The Secretary of State may by order confer additional functions on the Council.

(4) The power conferred by subsection (3) does not include power to confer on the Council any functions with respect to the investigation of any complaint which may be the subject of proceedings under this Act.

(5) In discharging its duties under this section, the Council shall in particular have regard to –
(a) the extent and nature of the benefits which would be likely to result from the implementation of any recommendation which it makes; and
(b) the likely cost of implementing any such recommendation.

(6) Where the Council makes any recommendation in the discharge of any of its functions under this section it shall, if it is reasonably practicable to do so, make an assessment of –
(a) the likely cost of implementing the recommendation; and
(b) the likely financial benefits which would result from implementing it.

(7) Where the Council proposes to give the Secretary of State advice on a matter, it shall before doing so –
(a) consult any body –
(i) established by any enactment or by a Minister of the Crown for the purpose of giving advice in relation to disability, or any aspect of disability; and
(ii) having functions in relation to the matter to which the advice relates;
(b) consult such other persons as it considers appropriate; and
(c) have regard to any representations made to it as a result of any such consultations.

(8) Schedule 5 makes further provision with respect to the Council, including provision about its membership.

(9) The power conferred on the Council by subsection (2) to give advice on its own initiative does not include power to give advice –
(a) by virtue of paragraph (a) or (b), in respect of any matter which relates to the operation of any provision of or arrangements made under –
(i) the [1944 c. 10.] [1958 c. 33.] Disabled Persons (Employment) Acts 1944 and 1958;
(ii) the [1973 c. 50.] Employment and Training Act 1973;
(iii) the [1978 c. 44.] Employment Protection (Consolidation) Act 1978; or
(iv) section 2(3) of the [1990 c. 35.] Enterprise and New Towns (Scotland) Act 1990; or
(b) by virtue of paragraph (c), in respect of any matter arising under Part II or section 53, 54, 56 or 61.

(10) Subsection (9) shall not have effect at any time when there is neither a national advisory council established under section 17(1)(a) of the Disabled Persons (Employment) Act 1944 nor any person appointed to act generally under section 60(1) of this Act.

Codes of practice prepared by the Council

51. (1) It shall be the duty of the Council, when asked to do so by the Secretary of State –
(a) to prepare proposals for a code of practice dealing with the matters to which the Secretary of State's request relates; or
(b) to review a code and, if it considers it appropriate, propose alterations.

(2) The Secretary of State may, in accordance with the procedural provisions of section 52, issue codes of practice in response to proposals made by the Council under this section.

(3) A failure on the part of any person to observe any provision of a code does not of itself make that person liable to any proceedings.

(4) A code is admissible in evidence in any proceedings under this Act before an industrial tribunal, a county court or a sheriff court.

(5) If any provision of a code appears to a tribunal or court to be relevant to any question arising in any proceedings under this Act, it shall be taken into account in determining that question.

(6) In this section and section 52 "code" means a code issued by the Secretary of State under this section and includes a code which has been altered and re-issued.

Further provision about codes issued under section 51

52. (1) In this section "proposal" means a proposal made by the Council to the Secretary of State under section 51.

(2) In preparing any proposal, the Council shall consult –

(a) such persons (if any) as the Secretary of State has specified in making his request to the Council; and

(b) such other persons (if any) as the Council considers appropriate.

(3) Before making any proposal, the Council shall publish a draft, consider any representations made to it about the draft and, if it thinks it appropriate, modify its proposal in the light of any of those representations.

(4) Where the Council makes any proposal, the Secretary of State may –

(a) approve it;

(b) approve it subject to such modifications as he considers appropriate; or

(c) refuse to approve it.

(5) Where the Secretary of State approves any proposal (with or without modifications), he shall prepare a draft of the proposed code and lay it before each House of Parliament.

(6) If, within the 40-day period, either House resolves not to approve the draft, the Secretary of State shall take no further steps in relation to the proposed code.

(7) If no such resolution is made within the 40-day period, the Secretary of State shall issue the code in the form of his draft.

(8) The code shall come into force on such date as the Secretary of State may appoint by order.

(9) Subsection (6) does not prevent a new draft of the proposed code from being laid before Parliament.

(10) If the Secretary of State refuses to approve a proposal, he shall give the Council a written statement of his reasons for not approving it.

(11) The Secretary of State may by order revoke a code.

(12) In this section "40-day period" , in relation to the draft of a proposed code, means –

(a) if the draft is laid before one House on a day later than the day on which it is laid before the other House, the period of 40 days beginning with the later of the two days, and
(b) in any other case, the period of 40 days beginning with the day on which the draft is laid before each House,

no account being taken of any period during which Parliament is dissolved or prorogued or during which both Houses are adjourned for more than four days.

PART VII

Supplemental

Codes of practice prepared by the Secretary of State

53. (1) The Secretary of State may issue codes of practice containing such practical guidance as he considers appropriate with a view to –
(a) eliminating discrimination in the field of employment against disabled persons and persons who have had a disability; or
(b) encouraging good practice in relation to the employment of disabled persons and persons who have had a disability.

(2) The Secretary of State may from time to time revise the whole or any part of a code and re-issue it.

(3) Without prejudice to subsection (1), a code may include practical guidance as to –
(a) the circumstances in which it would be reasonable, having regard in particular to the costs involved, for a person to be expected to make adjustments in favour of a disabled person or a person who has had a disability; or
(b) what steps it is reasonably practicable for employers to take for the purpose of preventing their employees from doing, in the course of their employment, anything which is made unlawful by this Act.

(4) A failure on the part of any person to observe any provision of a code does not of itself make that person liable to any proceedings.

(5) A code is admissible in evidence in any proceedings under this Act before an industrial tribunal, a county court or a sheriff court.

(6) If any provision of a code appears to a tribunal or court to be relevant to any question arising in any proceedings under this Act, it shall be taken into account in determining that question.

(7) In this section and section 54 "code" means a code issued by the Secretary of State under this section and includes a code which has been revised and re-issued.

(8) In subsection (1)(a), "discrimination in the field of employment" includes discrimination of a kind mentioned in section 12 or 13.

(9) In subsections (1)(b) and (3), "employment" includes contract work (as defined by section 12(6)).

Further provision about codes issued under section 53

54. (1) In preparing a draft of any code under section 53, the Secretary of State shall consult such organisations representing the interests of employers or of disabled persons in, or seeking, employment as he considers appropriate.

(2) Where the Secretary of State proposes to issue a code, he shall publish a draft of it, consider any representations that are made to him about the draft and, if he thinks it appropriate, modify his proposals in the light of any of those representations.

(3) If the Secretary of State decides to proceed with a proposed code, he shall lay a draft of it before each House of Parliament.

(4) If, within the 40-day period, either House resolves not to approve the draft, the Secretary of State shall take no further steps in relation to the proposed code.

(5) If no such resolution is made within the 40-day period, the Secretary of State shall issue the code in the form of his draft.

(6) The code shall come into force on such date as the Secretary of State may appoint by order.

(7) Subsection (4) does not prevent a new draft of the proposed code from being laid before Parliament.

(8) The Secretary of State may by order revoke a code.

(9) In this section "40-day period" , in relation to the draft of a proposed code, means –

(a) if the draft is laid before one House on a day later than the day on which it is laid before the other House, the period of 40 days beginning with the later of the two days, and

(b) in any other case, the period of 40 days beginning with the day on which the draft is laid before each House,

no account being taken of any period during which Parliament is dissolved or prorogued or during which both Houses are adjourned for more than four days.

Victimisation

55. (1) For the purposes of Part II or Part III, a person ("A") discriminates against another person ("B") if –

(a) he treats B less favourably than he treats or would treat other persons whose circumstances are the same as B's; and

(b) he does so for a reason mentioned in subsection (2).

(2) The reasons are that –

(a) B has –

(i) brought proceedings against A or any other person under this Act; or

(ii) given evidence or information in connection with such proceedings brought by any person; or

(iii) otherwise done anything under this Act in relation to A or any other person; or

(iv) alleged that A or any other person has (whether or not the allegation so states) contravened this Act; or

(b) A believes or suspects that B has done or intends to do any of those things.

(3) Where B is a disabled person, or a person who has had a disability, the disability in question shall be disregarded in comparing his circumstances with those of any other person for the purposes of subsection (1)(a).

(4) Subsection (1) does not apply to treatment of a person because of an allegation made by him if the allegation was false and not made in good faith.

Help for persons suffering discrimination

56. (1) For the purposes of this section –

(a) a person who considers that he may have been discriminated against, in contravention of any provision of Part II, is referred to as "the complainant" ; and

(b) a person against whom the complainant may decide to make, or has made, a complaint under Part II is referred to as "the respondent" .

(2) The Secretary of State shall, with a view to helping the complainant to decide whether to make a complaint against the respondent and, if he does so, to formulate and present his case in the most effective manner, by order prescribe –

(a) forms by which the complainant may question the respondent on his reasons for doing any relevant act, or on any other matter which is or may be relevant; and

(b) forms by which the respondent may if he so wishes reply to any questions.

(3) Where the complainant questions the respondent in accordance with forms prescribed by an order under subsection (2) –

(a) the question, and any reply by the respondent (whether in accordance with such an order or not), shall be admissible as evidence in any proceedings under Part II;

(b) if it appears to the tribunal in any such proceedings –

(i) that the respondent deliberately, and without reasonable excuse, omitted to reply within a reasonable period, or

(ii) that the respondent's reply is evasive or equivocal, it may draw any inference which it considers it just and equitable to draw, including an inference that the respondent has contravened a provision of Part II.

(4) The Secretary of State may by order prescribe –

(a) the period within which questions must be duly served in order to be admissible under subsection (3)(a); and

(b) the manner in which a question, and any reply by the respondent, may be duly served.

(5) This section is without prejudice to any other enactment or rule of law regulating interlocutory and preliminary matters in proceedings before an industrial tribunal, and has effect subject to any enactment or rule of law regulating the admissibility of evidence in such proceedings.

Aiding unlawful acts

57. (1) A person who knowingly aids another person to do an act made unlawful by this Act is to be treated for the purposes of this Act as himself doing the same kind of unlawful act.

(2) For the purposes of subsection (1), an employee or agent for whose act the employer or principal is liable under section 58 (or would be so liable but for section 58(5)) shall be taken to have aided the employer or principal to do the act.

(3) For the purposes of this section, a person does not knowingly aid another to do an unlawful act if –
   (a) he acts in reliance on a statement made to him by that other person that, because of any provision of this Act, the act would not be unlawful; and
   (b) it is reasonable for him to rely on the statement.

(4) A person who knowingly or recklessly makes such a statement which is false or misleading in a material respect is guilty of an offence.

(5) Any person guilty of an offence under subsection (4) shall be liable on summary conviction to a fine not exceeding level 5 on the standard scale.

Liability of employers and principals

58. (1) Anything done by a person in the course of his employment shall be treated for the purposes of this Act as also done by his employer, whether or not it was done with the employer's knowledge or approval.

(2) Anything done by a person as agent for another person with the authority of that other person shall be treated for the purposes of this Act as also done by that other person.

(3) Subsection (2) applies whether the authority was –
   (a) express or implied; or
   (b) given before or after the act in question was done.

(4) Subsections (1) and (2) do not apply in relation to an offence under section 57(4).

(5) In proceedings under this Act against any person in respect of an act alleged to have been done by an employee of his, it shall be a defence for that person to prove that he took such steps as were reasonably practicable to prevent the employee from –
   (a) doing that act; or
   (b) doing, in the course of his employment, acts of that description.

Statutory authority and national security etc.

59. (1) Nothing in this Act makes unlawful any act done –
   (a) in pursuance of any enactment; or
   (b) in pursuance of any instrument made by a Minister of the Crown under any enactment; or
   (c) to comply with any condition or requirement imposed by a Minister of the Crown (whether before or after the passing of this Act) by virtue of any enactment.

(2) In subsection (1) "enactment" includes one passed or made after the date on which this Act is passed and "instrument" includes one made after that date.

(3) Nothing in this Act makes unlawful any act done for the purpose of safeguarding national security.

PART VIII

Miscellaneous

Appointment by Secretary of State of advisers

60. (1) The Secretary of State may appoint such persons as he thinks fit to advise or assist him in connection with matters relating to the employment of disabled persons and persons who have had a disability.

(2) Persons may be appointed by the Secretary of State to act generally or in relation to a particular area or locality.

(3) The Secretary of State may pay to any person appointed under this section such allowances and compensation for loss of earnings as he considers appropriate.

(4) The approval of the Treasury is required for any payment under this section.

(5) In subsection (1) "employment" includes self-employment.

(6) The Secretary of State may by order –

(a) provide for section 17 of, and Schedule 2 to, the [1944 c. 10.] Disabled Persons (Employment) Act 1944 (national advisory council and district advisory committees) to cease to have effect –

(i) so far as concerns the national advisory council; or

(ii) so far as concerns district advisory committees; or

(b) repeal that section and Schedule.

(7) At any time before the coming into force of an order under paragraph (b) of subsection (6), section 17 of the Act of 1944 shall have effect as if in subsection (1), after "disabled persons" in each case there were inserted ", and persons who have had a disability," and as if at the end of the section there were added –

"(3) For the purposes of this section –

(a) a person is a disabled person if he is a disabled person for the purposes of the [1995 c. 50.] Disability Discrimination Act 1995; and

(b) "disability" has the same meaning as in that Act."

(8) At any time before the coming into force of an order under paragraph (a)(i) or (b) of subsection (6), section 16 of the [1970 c. 44.] Chronically Sick and Disabled Persons Act 1970 (which extends the functions of the national advisory council) shall have effect as if after "disabled persons" in each case there were inserted ", and persons who have had a disability," and as if at the end of the section there were added –

"(2) For the purposes of this section –

(a) a person is a disabled person if he is a disabled person for the purposes of the Disability Discrimination Act 1995; and

(b) "disability" has the same meaning as in that Act."

Amendment of Disabled Persons (Employment) Act 1944

61. (1) Section 15 of the [1944 c. 10.] Disabled Persons (Employment) Act 1944 (which gives the Secretary of state power to make arrangements for the provision of supported employment) is amended as set out in subsections (2) to (5).

(2) In subsection (1) –

(a) for "persons registered as handicapped by disablement" substitute "disabled persons"

(b) for "their disablement" substitute "their disability" and

(c) for "are not subject to disablement" substitute "do not have a disability".

(3) In subsection (2), for the words from "any of one or more companies" to "so required and prohibited" substitute "any company, association or body".

(4) After subsection (2) insert –

"(2A) The only kind of company which the Minister himself may form in exercising his powers under this section is a company which is –

(a) required by its constitution to apply its profits, if any, or other income in promoting its objects; and

(b) prohibited by its constitution from paying any dividend to its members."

(5) After subsection (5) insert –

"(5A) For the purposes of this section –

(a) a person is a disabled person if he is a disabled person for the purposes of the Disability Discrimination Act 1995; and

(b) "disability" has the same meaning as in that Act."

(6) The provisions of section 16 (preference to be given under section 15 of that Act to ex-service men and women) shall become subsection (1) of that section and at the end insert –

"and whose disability is due to that service.

(2) For the purposes of subsection (1) of this section, a disabled person's disability shall be treated as due to service of a particular kind only in such circumstances as may be prescribed."

(7) The following provisions of the Act of 1944 shall cease to have effect –

(a) section 1 (definition of "disabled person");

(b) sections 6 to 8 (the register of disabled persons);

(c) sections 9 to 11 (obligations on employers with substantial staffs to employ a quota of registered persons);

(d) section 12 (the designated employment scheme for persons registered as handicapped by disablement);

(e) section 13 (interpretation of provisions repealed by this Act);

(f) section 14 (records to be kept by employers);

(g) section 19 (proceedings in relation to offences); and

(h) section 21 (application as respects place of employment, and nationality).

(8) Any provision of subordinate legislation in which "disabled person" is defined by reference to the Act of 1944 shall be construed as if that expression had the same meaning as in this Act.

(9) Subsection (8) does not prevent the further amendment of any such provision by subordinate legislation.

Restriction of publicity: industrial tribunals

62. (1) This section applies to proceedings on a complaint under section 8 in which evidence of a personal nature is likely to be heard by the industrial tribunal hearing the complaint.

(2) The power of the Secretary of State to make regulations with respect to the procedure of industrial tribunals includes power to make provision in relation to proceedings to which this section applies for –

(a) enabling an industrial tribunal, on the application of the complainant or of its own motion, to make a restricted reporting order having effect (if not revoked earlier) until the promulgation of the tribunal's decision; and

(b) where a restricted reporting order is made in relation to a complaint which is being dealt with by the tribunal together with any other proceedings, enabling the tribunal to direct that the order is to apply also in relation to those other proceedings or such part of them as the tribunal may direct.

(3) If any identifying matter is published or included in a relevant programme in contravention of a restricted reporting order –
(a) in the case of publication in a newspaper or periodical, any proprietor, any editor and any publisher of the newspaper or periodical,
(b) in the case of publication in any other form, the person publishing the matter, and
(c) in the case of matter included in a relevant programme –
(i) any body corporate engaged in providing the service in which the programme is included, and
(ii) any person having functions in relation to the programme corresponding to those of an editor of a newspaper, shall be guilty of an offence and liable on summary conviction to a fine not exceeding level 5 on the standard scale.

(4) Where a person is charged with an offence under subsection (3), it is a defence to prove that at the time of the alleged offence –
(a) he was not aware, and
(b) he neither suspected nor had reason to suspect,
that the publication or programme in question was of, or included, the matter in question.

(5) Where an offence under subsection (3) committed by a body corporate is proved to have been committed with the consent or connivance of, or to be attributable to any neglect on the part of –
(a) a director, manager, secretary or other similar officer of the body corporate, or
(b) a person purporting to act in any such capacity,
he as well as the body corporate is guilty of the offence and liable to be proceeded against and punished accordingly.

(6) In relation to a body corporate whose affairs are managed by its members "director", in subsection (5), means a member of the body corporate.

(7) In this section –
"evidence of a personal nature" means any evidence of a medical, or other intimate, nature which might reasonably be assumed to be likely to cause significant embarrassment to the complainant if reported;
"identifying matter" means any matter likely to lead members of the public to identify the complainant or such other persons (if any) as may be named in the order;
"promulgation" has such meaning as may be prescribed by the regulations;
"relevant programme" means a programme included in a programme service, within the meaning of the [1990 c. 42.] Broadcasting Act 1990;
"restricted reporting order" means an order –
(a) made in exercise of the power conferred by regulations made by virtue of this section; and
(b) prohibiting the publication in Great Britain of identifying matter in a written publication available to the public or its inclusion in a relevant programme for reception in Great Britain; and
"written publication" includes a film, a soundtrack and any other record in permanent form but does not include an indictment or other document prepared for use in particular legal proceedings.

Restriction of publicity: Employment Appeal Tribunal

63. (1) This section applies to proceedings –

(a) on an appeal against a decision of an industrial tribunal to make, or not to make, a restricted reporting order, or

(b) on an appeal against any interlocutory decision of an industrial tribunal in proceedings in which the industrial tribunal has made a restricted reporting order which it has not revoked.

(2) The power of the Lord Chancellor to make rules with respect to the procedure of the Employment Appeal Tribunal includes power to make provision in relation to proceedings to which this section applies for –

(a) enabling the Tribunal, on the application of the complainant or of its own motion, to make a restricted reporting order having effect (if not revoked earlier) until the promulgation of the Tribunal's decision; and

(b) where a restricted reporting order is made in relation to an appeal which is being dealt with by the Tribunal together with any other proceedings, enabling the Tribunal to direct that the order is to apply also in relation to those other proceedings or such part of them as the Tribunal may direct.

(3) Subsections (3) to (6) of section 62 apply in relation to a restricted reporting order made by the Tribunal as they apply in relation to one made by an industrial tribunal.

(4) In subsection (1), "restricted reporting order" means an order which is a restricted reporting order for the purposes of section 62.

(5) In subsection (2), "restricted reporting order" means an order –

(a) made in exercise of the power conferred by rules made by virtue of this section; and

(b) prohibiting the publication in Great Britain of identifying matter in a written publication available to the public or its inclusion in a relevant programme for reception in Great Britain.

(6) In this section –

"complainant" means the person who made the complaint to which the proceedings before the Tribunal relate;

"identifying matter", "written publication" and "relevant programme" have the same meaning as in section 62; and

"promulgation" has such meaning as may be prescribed by the rules.

Application to Crown etc.

64. (1) This Act applies –

(a) to an act done by or for purposes of a Minister of the Crown or government department, or

(b) to an act done on behalf of the Crown by a statutory body, or a person holding a statutory office,

as it applies to an act done by a private person.

(2) Subject to subsection (5), Part II applies to service –

(a) for purposes of a Minister of the Crown or government department, other than service of a person holding a statutory office, or

(b) on behalf of the Crown for purposes of a person holding a statutory office or purposes of a statutory body,

as it applies to employment by a private person.

(3) The provisions of Parts II to IV of the 1947 Act apply to proceedings against the Crown under this Act as they apply to Crown proceedings in England and

Wales; but section 20 of that Act (removal of proceedings from county court to High Court) does not apply.

(4) The provisions of Part V of the 1947 Act apply to proceedings against the Crown under this Act as they apply to proceedings in Scotland which by virtue of that Part are treated as civil proceedings by or against the Crown; but the proviso to section 44 of that Act (removal of proceedings from the sheriff court to the Court of Session) does not apply.

(5) Part II does not apply to service –

(a) as a member of the Ministry of Defence Police, the British Transport Police, the Royal Parks Constabulary or the United Kingdom Atomic Energy Authority Constabulary;

(b) as a prison officer; or

(c) for purposes of a Minister of the Crown or government department having functions with respect to defence as a person who is or may be required by his terms of service to engage in fire fighting.

(6) Part II does not apply to service as a member of a fire brigade who is or may be required by his terms of service to engage in fire fighting.

(7) It is hereby declared (for the avoidance of doubt) that Part II does not apply to service in any of the naval, military or air forces of the Crown.

(8) In this section –

"the 1947 Act" means the [1947 c. 44.] Crown Proceedings Act 1947;

"British Transport Police" means the constables appointed, or deemed to have been appointed, under section 53 of the [1949 c. xxix.] British Transport Commission Act 1949;

"Crown proceedings" means proceedings which, by virtue of section 23 of the 1947 Act, are treated for the purposes of Part II of that Act as civil proceedings by or against the Crown;

"fire brigade" means a fire brigade maintained in pursuance of the [1947 c. 41.] Fire Services Act 1947;

"Ministry of Defence Police" means the force established under section 1 of the [1987 c. 4.] Ministry of Defence Police Act 1987;

"prison officer" means a person who is a prison officer within the meaning of section 127 of the [1994 c. 33.] Criminal Justice and Public Order Act 1994, apart from those who are custody officers within the meaning of Part I of that Act;

"Royal Parks Constabulary" means the park constables appointed under the [1872 c. 15.] Parks Regulation Act 1872;

"service for purposes of a Minister of the Crown or government department" does not include service in any office for the time being mentioned in Schedule 2 (Ministerial offices) to the [1975 c. 24.] House of Commons Disqualification Act 1975;

"statutory body" means a body set up by or under an enactment;

"statutory office" means an office so set up; and

"United Kingdom Atomic Energy Authority Constabulary" means the special constables appointed under section 3 of the [1923 c. 11.] Special Constables Act 1923 on the nomination of the United Kingdom Atomic Energy Authority.

Application to Parliament

65. (1) This Act applies to an act done by or for purposes of the House of Lords or the House of Commons as it applies to an act done by a private person.

(2) For the purposes of the application of Part II in relation to the House of Commons, the Corporate Officer of that House shall be treated as the employer of a person who is (or would be) a relevant member of the House of Commons staff for the purposes of section 139 of the [1978 c. 44.] Employment Protection (Consolidation) Act 1978.

(3) Except as provided in subsection (4), for the purposes of the application of sections 19 to 21, the provider of services is –

(a) as respects the House of Lords, the Corporate Officer of that House; and

(b) as respects the House of Commons, the Corporate Officer of that House.

(4) Where the service in question is access to and use of any place in the Palace of Westminster which members of the public are permitted to enter, the Corporate Officers of both Houses jointly are the provider of that service.

(5) Nothing in any rule of law or the law or practice of Parliament prevents proceedings being instituted before an industrial tribunal under Part II or before any court under Part III.

Government appointments outside Part II

66. (1) Subject to regulations under subsection (3), this section applies to any appointment made by a Minister of the Crown or government department to an office or post where Part II does not apply in relation to the appointment.

(2) In making the appointment, and in making arrangements for determining to whom the office or post should be offered, the Minister of the Crown or government department shall not act in a way which would contravene Part II if he or the department were the employer for the purposes of this Act.

(3) Regulations may provide for this section not to apply to such appointments as may be prescribed.

Regulations and orders

67. (1) Any power under this Act to make regulations or orders shall be exercisable by statutory instrument.

(2) Any such power may be exercised to make different provision for different cases, including different provision for different areas or localities.

(3) Any such power includes power –

(a) to make such incidental, supplemental, consequential or transitional provision as appears to the Secretary of State to be expedient; and

(b) to provide for a person to exercise a discretion in dealing with any matter.

(4) No order shall be made under section 50(3) unless a draft of the statutory instrument containing the order has been laid before Parliament and approved by a resolution of each House.

(5) Any other statutory instrument made under this Act, other than one made under section 3(9), 52(8), 54(6) or 70(3), shall be subject to annulment in pursuance of a resolution of either House of Parliament.

(6) Subsection (1) does not require an order under section 43 which applies only to a specified vehicle, or to vehicles of a specified person, to be made by

statutory instrument but such an order shall be as capable of being amended or revoked as an order which is made by statutory instrument.

(7) Nothing in section 34(4), 40(6) or 46(5) affects the powers conferred by subsections (2) and (3).

Interpretation

68. (1) In this Act –

"accessibility certificate" means a certificate issued under section 41(1)(a);

"act" includes a deliberate omission;

"approval certificate" means a certificate issued under section 42(4);

"benefits", in Part II, has the meaning given in section 4(4);

"conciliation officer" means a person designated under section 211 of the [1992 c. 52.] Trade Union and Labour Relations (Consolidation) Act 1992;

"employment" means, subject to any prescribed provision, employment under a contract of service or of apprenticeship or a contract personally to do any work, and related expressions are to be construed accordingly;

"employment at an establishment in Great Britain" is to be construed in accordance with subsections (2) to (5);

"enactment" includes subordinate legislation and any Order in Council;

"licensing authority" means –

(a) in relation to the area to which the [1869 c. 115.] Metropolitan Public Carriage Act 1869 applies, the Secretary of State or the holder of any office for the time being designated by the Secretary of State; or

(b) in relation to any other area in England and Wales, the authority responsible for licensing taxis in that area;

"mental impairment" does not have the same meaning as in the [1983 c. 20.] Mental Health Act 1983 or the [1984 c. 36.] Mental Health (Scotland) Act 1984 but the fact that an impairment would be a mental impairment for the purposes of either of those Acts does not prevent it from being a mental impairment for the purposes of this Act;

"Minister of the Crown" includes the Treasury;

"occupational pension scheme" has the same meaning as in the [1993 c. 48.] Pension Schemes Act 1993;

"premises" includes land of any description;

"prescribed" means prescribed by regulations;

"profession" includes any vocation or occupation;

"provider of services" has the meaning given in section 19(2)(b);

"public service vehicle" and "regulated public service vehicle" have the meaning given in section 40;

"PSV accessibility regulations" means regulations made under section 40(1);

"rail vehicle" and "regulated rail vehicle" have the meaning given in section 46;

"rail vehicle accessibility regulations" means regulations made under section 46(1);

"regulations" means regulations made by the Secretary of State;

"section 6 duty" means any duty imposed by or under section 6;

"section 15 duty" means any duty imposed by or under section 15;

"section 21 duty" means any duty imposed by or under section 21;

"subordinate legislation" has the same meaning as in section 21 of the [1978 c. 30.] Interpretation Act 1978;

"taxi" and "regulated taxi" have the meaning given in section 32;

"taxi accessibility regulations" means regulations made under section 32(1);
"trade" includes any business;
"trade organisation" has the meaning given in section 13;
"vehicle examiner" means an examiner appointed under section 66A of the [1988 c. 52.] Road Traffic Act 1988.

(2) Where an employee does his work wholly or mainly outside Great Britain, his employment is not to be treated as being work at an establishment in Great Britain even if he does some of his work at such an establishment.

(3) Except in prescribed cases, employment on board a ship, aircraft or hovercraft is to be regarded as not being employment at an establishment in Great Britain.

(4) Employment of a prescribed kind, or in prescribed circumstances, is to be regarded as not being employment at an establishment in Great Britain.

(5) Where work is not done at an establishment it shall be treated as done –
(a) at the establishment from which it is done; or
(b) where it is not done from any establishment, at the establishment with which it has the closest connection.

Financial provisions

69. There shall be paid out of money provided by Parliament –
(a) any expenditure incurred by a Minister of the Crown under this Act;
(b) any increase attributable to this Act in the sums payable out of money so provided under or by virtue of any other enactment.

Short title, commencement, extent etc.

70. (1) This Act may be cited as the Disability Discrimination Act 1995.

(2) This section (apart from subsections (4), (5) and (7)) comes into force on the passing of this Act.

(3) The other provisions of this Act come into force on such day as the Secretary of State may by order appoint and different days may be appointed for different purposes.

(4) Schedule 6 makes consequential amendments.

(5) The repeals set out in Schedule 7 shall have effect.

(6) This Act extends to Northern Ireland, but in their application to Northern Ireland the provisions of this Act mentioned in Schedule 8 shall have effect subject to the modifications set out in that Schedule.

(7) In Part II of Schedule 1 to the [1975 c. 24.] House of Commons Disqualification Act 1975 and in Part II of Schedule 1 to the [1975 c. 25.] Northern Ireland Assembly Disqualification Act 1975 (bodies whose members are disqualified) in each case insert at the appropriate places –
"The National Disability Council."
"The Northern Ireland Disability Council."

(8) Consultations which are required by any provision of this Act to be held by the Secretary of State may be held by him before the coming into force of that provision.

SCHEDULES

SCHEDULE 1

Section 1(1)

Provisions Supplementing Section 1

Impairment

1. (1) "Mental impairment" includes an impairment resulting from or consisting of a mental illness only if the illness is a clinically well-recognised illness.

(2) Regulations may make provision, for the purposes of this Act –

(a) for conditions of a prescribed description to be treated as amounting to impairments;

(b) for conditions of a prescribed description to be treated as not amounting to impairments.

(3) Regulations made under sub-paragraph (2) may make provision as to the meaning of "condition" for the purposes of those regulations.

Long-term effects

2. (1) The effect of an impairment is a long-term effect if –

(a) it has lasted at least 12 months;

(b) the period for which it lasts is likely to be at least 12 months; or

(c) it is likely to last for the rest of the life of the person affected.

(2) Where an impairment ceases to have a substantial adverse effect on a person's ability to carry out normal day-to-day activities, it is to be treated as continuing to have that effect if that effect is likely to recur.

(3) For the purposes of sub-paragraph (2), the likelihood of an effect recurring shall be disregarded in prescribed circumstances.

(4) Regulations may prescribe circumstances in which, for the purposes of this Act –

(a) an effect which would not otherwise be a long-term effect is to be treated as such an effect; or

(b) an effect which would otherwise be a long-term effect is to be treated as not being such an effect.

Severe disfigurement

3. (1) An impairment which consists of a severe disfigurement is to be treated as having a substantial adverse effect on the ability of the person concerned to carry out normal day-to-day activities.

(2) Regulations may provide that in prescribed circumstances a severe disfigurement is not to be treated as having that effect.

(3) Regulations under sub-paragraph (2) may, in particular, make provision with respect to deliberately acquired disfigurements.

Normal day-to-day activities

4. (1) An impairment is to be taken to affect the ability of the person concerned to carry out normal day-to-day activities only if it affects one of the following –

(a) mobility;

(b) manual dexterity;

(c) physical co-ordination;

(d) continence;

(e) ability to lift, carry or otherwise move everyday objects;
(f) speech, hearing or eyesight;
(g) memory or ability to concentrate, learn or understand; or
(h) perception of the risk of physical danger.

(2) Regulations may prescribe –
(a) circumstances in which an impairment which does not have an effect falling within sub-paragraph (1) is to be taken to affect the ability of the person concerned to carry out normal day-to-day activities;
(b) circumstances in which an impairment which has an effect falling within sub-paragraph (1) is to be taken not to affect the ability of the person concerned to carry out normal day-to-day activities.

Substantial adverse effects

5. Regulations may make provision for the purposes of this Act –
(a) for an effect of a prescribed kind on the ability of a person to carry out normal day-to-day activities to be treated as a substantial adverse effect;
(b) for an effect of a prescribed kind on the ability of a person to carry out normal day-to-day activities to be treated as not being a substantial adverse effect.

Effect of medical treatment

6. (1) An impairment which would be likely to have a substantial adverse effect on the ability of the person concerned to carry out normal day-to-day activities, but for the fact that measures are being taken to treat or correct it, is to be treated as having that effect.

(2) In sub-paragraph (1) "measures" includes, in particular, medical treatment and the use of a prosthesis or other aid.

(3) Sub-paragraph (1) does not apply –
(a) in relation to the impairment of a person's sight, to the extent that the impairment is, in his case, correctable by spectacles or contact lenses or in such other ways as may be prescribed; or
(b) in relation to such other impairments as may be prescribed, in such circumstances as may be prescribed.

Persons deemed to be disabled

7. (1) Sub-paragraph (2) applies to any person whose name is, both on 12th January 1995 and on the date when this paragraph comes into force, in the register of disabled persons maintained under section 6 of the [1944 c. 10.] Disabled Persons (Employment) Act 1944.

(2) That person is to be deemed –
(a) during the initial period, to have a disability, and hence to be a disabled person; and
(b) afterwards, to have had a disability and hence to have been a disabled person during that period.

(3) A certificate of registration shall be conclusive evidence, in relation to the person with respect to whom it was issued, of the matters certified.

(4) Unless the contrary is shown, any document purporting to be a certificate of registration shall be taken to be such a certificate and to have been validly issued.

(5) Regulations may provide for prescribed descriptions of person to be deemed to have disabilities, and hence to be disabled persons, for the purposes of this Act.

(6) Regulations may prescribe circumstances in which a person who has been deemed to be a disabled person by the provisions of sub-paragraph (1) or regulations made under sub-paragraph (5) is to be treated as no longer being deemed to be such a person.

(7) In this paragraph –
"certificate of registration" means a certificate issued under regulations made under section 6 of the Act of 1944; and
"initial period" means the period of three years beginning with the date on which this paragraph comes into force.

Progressive conditions

8. (1) Where –
(a) a person has a progressive condition (such as cancer, multiple sclerosis or muscular dystrophy or infection by the human immunodeficiency virus),
(b) as a result of that condition, he has an impairment which has (or had) an effect on his ability to carry out normal day-to-day activities, but
(c) that effect is not (or was not) a substantial adverse effect,
he shall be taken to have an impairment which has such a substantial adverse effect if the condition is likely to result in his having such an impairment.

(2) Regulations may make provision, for the purposes of this paragraph –
(a) for conditions of a prescribed description to be treated as being progressive;
(b) for conditions of a prescribed description to be treated as not being progressive.

SCHEDULE 2

Section 2(2)

Past Disabilities

1. The modifications referred to in section 2 are as follows.

2. References in Parts II and III to a disabled person are to be read as references to a person who has had a disability.

3. In section 6(1), after "not disabled" insert "and who have not had a disability".

4. In section 6(6), for "has" substitute "has had".

5. For paragraph 2(1) to (3) of Schedule 1, substitute –
"(1) The effect of an impairment is a long-term effect if it has lasted for at least 12 months.
(2) Where an impairment ceases to have a substantial adverse effect on a person's ability to carry out normal day-to-day activities, it is to be treated as continuing to have that effect if that effect recurs.
(3) For the purposes of sub-paragraph (2), the recurrence of an effect shall be disregarded in prescribed circumstances."

SCHEDULE 3

Sections 8(8) and 25(6)

Enforcement and Procedure

Part I

Employment

Conciliation

1. (1) Where a complaint is presented to an industrial tribunal under section 8 and a copy of it is sent to a conciliation officer, he shall –

(a) if requested to do so by the complainant and respondent, or

(b) if he considers that he has a reasonable prospect of success,

try to promote a settlement of the complaint without its being determined by an industrial tribunal.

(2) Where a person is contemplating presenting such a complaint, a conciliation officer shall, if asked to do so by the potential complainant or potential respondent, try to promote a settlement.

(3) The conciliation officer shall, where appropriate, have regard to the desirability of encouraging the use of other procedures available for the settlement of grievances.

(4) Anything communicated to a conciliation officer in a case in which he is acting under this paragraph shall not be admissible in evidence in any proceedings before an industrial tribunal except with the consent of the person who communicated it.

Restriction on proceedings for breach of Part II

2. (1) Except as provided by section 8, no civil or criminal proceedings may be brought against any person in respect of an act merely because the act is unlawful under Part II.

(2) Sub-paragraph (1) does not prevent the making of an application for judicial review.

Period within which proceedings must be brought

3. (1) An industrial tribunal shall not consider a complaint under section 8 unless it is presented before the end of the period of three months beginning when the act complained of was done.

(2) A tribunal may consider any such complaint which is out of time if, in all the circumstances of the case, it considers that it is just and equitable to do so.

(3) For the purposes of sub-paragraph (1) –

(a) where an unlawful act of discrimination is attributable to a term in a contract, that act is to be treated as extending throughout the duration of the contract;

(b) any act extending over a period shall be treated as done at the end of that period; and

(c) a deliberate omission shall be treated as done when the person in question decided upon it.

(4) In the absence of evidence establishing the contrary, a person shall be taken for the purposes of this paragraph to decide upon an omission –

(a) when he does an act inconsistent with doing the omitted act; or

(b) if he has done no such inconsistent act, when the period expires within which he might reasonably have been expected to do the omitted act if it was to be done.

Evidence

4. (1) In any proceedings under section 8, a certificate signed by or on behalf of a Minister of the Crown and certifying –

(a) that any conditions or requirements specified in the certificate were imposed by a Minister of the Crown and were in operation at a time or throughout a time so specified, or

(b) that an act specified in the certificate was done for the purpose of safeguarding national security,

shall be conclusive evidence of the matters certified.

(2) A document purporting to be such a certificate shall be received in evidence and, unless the contrary is proved, be deemed to be such a certificate.

Part II

Discrimination in Other Areas

Restriction on proceedings for breach of Part III

5. (1) Except as provided by section 25 no civil or criminal proceedings may be brought against any person in respect of an act merely because the act is unlawful under Part III.

(2) Sub-paragraph (1) does not prevent the making of an application for judicial review.

Period within which proceedings must be brought

6. (1) A county court or a sheriff court shall not consider a claim under section 25 unless proceedings in respect of the claim are instituted before the end of the period of six months beginning when the act complained of was done.

(2) Where, in relation to proceedings or prospective proceedings under section 25, a person appointed in connection with arrangements under section 28 is approached before the end of the period of six months mentioned in sub-paragraph (1), the period allowed by that sub-paragraph shall be extended by two months.

(3) A court may consider any claim under section 25 which is out of time if, in all the circumstances of the case, it considers that it is just and equitable to do so.

(4) For the purposes of sub-paragraph (1) –

(a) where an unlawful act of discrimination is attributable to a term in a contract, that act is to be treated as extending throughout the duration of the contract;

(b) any act extending over a period shall be treated as done at the end of that period; and

(c) a deliberate omission shall be treated as done when the person in question decided upon it.

(5) In the absence of evidence establishing the contrary, a person shall be taken for the purposes of this paragraph to decide upon an omission –

(a) when he does an act inconsistent with doing the omitted act; or

(b) if he has done no such inconsistent act, when the period expires within which he might reasonably have been expected to do the omitted act if it was to be done.

Compensation for injury to feelings

7. In any proceedings under section 25, the amount of any damages awarded as compensation for injury to feelings shall not exceed the prescribed amount.

Evidence

8. (1) In any proceedings under section 25, a certificate signed by or on behalf of a Minister of the Crown and certifying –

(a) that any conditions or requirements specified in the certificate were imposed by a Minister of the Crown and were in operation at a time or throughout a time so specified, or

(b) that an act specified in the certificate was done for the purpose of safeguarding national security,

shall be conclusive evidence of the matters certified.

(2) A document purporting to be such a certificate shall be received in evidence and, unless the contrary is proved, be deemed to be such a certificate.

SCHEDULE 4

Sections 16(5) and 27(5)

Premises Occupied Under Leases

Part I

Occupation by Employer or Trade Organisation

Failure to obtain consent to alteration

1. If any question arises as to whether the occupier has failed to comply with the section 6 or section 15 duty, by failing to make a particular alteration to the premises, any constraint attributable to the fact that he occupies the premises under a lease is to be ignored unless he has applied to the lessor in writing for consent to the making of the alteration.

Joining lessors in proceedings under section 8

2. (1) In any proceedings under section 8, in a case to which section 16 applies, the complainant or the occupier may ask the tribunal hearing the complaint to direct that the lessor be joined or sisted as a party to the proceedings.

(2) The request shall be granted if it is made before the hearing of the complaint begins.

(3) The tribunal may refuse the request if it is made after the hearing of the complaint begins.

(4) The request may not be granted if it is made after the tribunal has determined the complaint.

(5) Where a lessor has been so joined or sisted as a party to the proceedings, the tribunal may determine –

(a) whether the lessor has –

(i) refused consent to the alteration, or

(ii) consented subject to one or more conditions, and

(b) if so, whether the refusal or any of the conditions was unreasonable,

(6) If, under sub-paragraph (5), the tribunal determines that the refusal or any of the conditions was unreasonable it may take one or more of the following steps –
(a) make such declaration as it considers appropriate;
(b) make an order authorising the occupier to make the alteration specified in the order;
(c) order the lessor to pay compensation to the complainant.

(7) An order under sub-paragraph (6)(b) may require the occupier to comply with conditions specified in the order.

(8) Any step taken by the tribunal under sub-paragraph (6) may be in substitution for, or in addition to, any step taken by the tribunal under section 8(2).

(9) If the tribunal orders the lessor to pay compensation it may not make an order under section 8(2) ordering the occupier to do so.

Regulations

3. Regulations may make provision as to circumstances in which –
(a) a lessor is to be taken, for the purposes of section 16 and this Part of this Schedule to have –
(i) withheld his consent;
(ii) withheld his consent unreasonably;
(iii) acted reasonably in withholding his consent;
(b) a condition subject to which a lessor has given his consent is to be taken to be reasonable;
(c) a condition subject to which a lessor has given his consent is to be taken to be unreasonable.

Sub-leases etc.

4. The Secretary of State may by regulations make provision supplementing, or modifying, the provision made by section 16 or any provision made by or under this Part of this Schedule in relation to cases where the occupier occupies premises under a sub-lease or sub-tenancy.

Part II

Occupation by Provider of Services

Failure to obtain consent to alteration

5. If any question arises as to whether the occupier has failed to comply with the section 21 duty, by failing to make a particular alteration to premises, any constraint attributable to the fact that he occupies the premises under a lease is to be ignored unless he has applied to the lessor in writing for consent to the making of the alteration.

Reference to court

6. (1) If the occupier has applied in writing to the lessor for consent to the alteration and –
(a) that consent has been refused, or
(b) the lessor has made his consent subject to one or more conditions,
the occupier or a disabled person who has an interest in the proposed alteration to the premises being made, may refer the matter to a county court or, in Scotland, to the sheriff.

(2) In the following provisions of this Schedule "court" includes "sheriff".

(3) On such a reference the court shall determine whether the lessor's refusal was unreasonable or (as the case may be) whether the condition is, or any of the conditions are, unreasonable.

(4) If the court determines –

(a) that the lessor's refusal was unreasonable, or

(b) that the condition is, or any of the conditions are, unreasonable,

it may make such declaration as it considers appropriate or an order authorising the occupier to make the alteration specified in the order.

(5) An order under sub-paragraph (4) may require the occupier to comply with conditions specified in the order.

Joining lessors in proceedings under section 25

7. (1) In any proceedings on a claim under section 25, in a case to which this Part of this Schedule applies, the plaintiff, the pursuer or the occupier concerned may ask the court to direct that the lessor be joined or sisted as a party to the proceedings.

(2) The request shall be granted if it is made before the hearing of the claim begins.

(3) The court may refuse the request if it is made after the hearing of the claim begins.

(4) The request may not be granted if it is made after the court has determined the claim.

(5) Where a lessor has been so joined or sisted as a party to the proceedings, the court may determine –

(a) whether the lessor has –

(i) refused consent to the alteration, or

(ii) consented subject to one or more conditions, and

(b) if so, whether the refusal or any of the conditions was unreasonable.

(6) If, under sub-paragraph (5), the court determines that the refusal or any of the conditions was unreasonable it may take one or more of the following steps –

(a) make such declaration as it considers appropriate;

(b) make an order authorising the occupier to make the alteration specified in the order;

(c) order the lessor to pay compensation to the complainant.

(7) An order under sub-paragraph (6)(b) may require the occupier to comply with conditions specified in the order.

(8) If the court orders the lessor to pay compensation it may not order the occupier to do so.

Regulations

8. Regulations may make provision as to circumstances in which –

(a) a lessor is to be taken, for the purposes of section 27 and this Part of this Schedule to have –

(i) withheld his consent;

(ii) withheld his consent unreasonably;

(iii) acted reasonably in withholding his consent;

(b) a condition subject to which a lessor has given his consent is to be taken to be reasonable;

(c) a condition subject to which a lessor has given his consent is to be taken to be unreasonable.

Sub-leases etc.

9. The Secretary of State may by regulations make provision supplementing, or modifying, the provision made by section 27 or any provision made by or under this Part of this Schedule in relation to cases where the occupier occupies premises under a sub-lease or sub-tenancy.

SCHEDULE 5

Section 50(8).

The National Disability Council

Status

1. (1) The Council shall be a body corporate.

(2) The Council is not the servant or agent of the Crown and does not enjoy any status, immunity or privilege of the Crown.

Procedure

2. The Council has power to regulate its own procedure (including power to determine its quorum).

Membership

3. (1) The Council shall consist of at least 10, but not more than 20, members.

(2) In this Schedule "member" , except in sub-paragraph (5)(b), means a member of the Council.

(3) Each member shall be appointed by the Secretary of State.

(4) The Secretary of State shall appoint one member to be chairman of the Council and another member to be its deputy chairman.

(5) The members shall be appointed from among persons who, in the opinion of the Secretary of State –

(a) have knowledge or experience of the needs of disabled persons or the needs of a particular group, or particular groups, of disabled persons;

(b) have knowledge or experience of the needs of persons who have had a disability or the needs of a particular group, or particular groups, of such persons; or

(c) are members of, or otherwise represent, professional bodies or bodies which represent industry or other business interests.

(6) Before appointing any member, the Secretary of State shall consult such persons as he considers appropriate.

(7) In exercising his powers of appointment, the Secretary of State shall try to secure that at all times at least half the membership of the Council consists of disabled persons, persons who have had a disability or the parents or guardians of disabled persons.

Term of office of members

4. (1) Each member shall be appointed for a term which does not exceed five years but shall otherwise hold and vacate his office in accordance with the terms of his appointment.

(2) A person shall not be prevented from being appointed as a member merely because he has previously been a member.

(3) Any member may at any time resign his office by written notice given to the Secretary of State.

(4) Regulations may make provision for the Secretary of State to remove a member from his office in such circumstances as may be prescribed.

Remuneration

5. (1) The Secretary of State may pay such remuneration or expenses to any member as he considers appropriate.

(2) The approval of the Treasury is required for any payment made under this paragraph.

Staff

6. The Secretary of State shall provide the Council with such staff as he considers appropriate.

Supplementary regulation-making power

7. The Secretary of State may by regulations make provision –

(a) as to the provision of information to the Council by the Secretary of State;

(b) as to the commissioning by the Secretary of State of research to be undertaken on behalf of the Council;

(c) as to the circumstances in which and conditions subject to which the Council may appoint any person as an adviser;

(d) as to the payment by the Secretary of State, with the approval of the Treasury, of expenses incurred by the Council.

Annual report

8. (1) As soon as is practicable after the end of each financial year, the Council shall report to the Secretary of State on its activities during the financial year to which the report relates.

(2) The Secretary of State shall lay a copy of every annual report of the Council before each House of Parliament and shall arrange for such further publication of the report as he considers appropriate.

SCHEDULE 6

Section 70(4).

Consequential Amendments

Employment and Training Act 1973 (c. 50)

1. In section 12(1) of the Employment and Training Act 1973 (duty of Secretary of State to give preference to ex-service men and women in exercising certain powers in respect of disabled persons) –

(a) for "persons registered as handicapped by disablement" substitute "disabled persons" and

(b) for the words after ""disabled person"" substitute "has the same meaning as in the Disability Discrimination Act 1995."

Employment Protection (Consolidation) Act 1978 (c. 44)

2. In section 136(1) of the Employment Protection (Consolidation) Act 1978 (appeals to Employment Appeal Tribunal), at the end insert –

" (ff) the Disability Discrimination Act 1995."

3. In paragraph 20 of Schedule 13 to that Act (reinstatement or re-engagement of dismissed employees), in sub-paragraph (3) –

(a) in the definition of "relevant complaint of dismissal", omit "or" and at the end insert "or a complaint under section 8 of the Disability Discrimination Act 1995 arising out of a dismissal"

(b) in the definition of "relevant conciliation powers", omit "or" and at the end insert "or paragraph 1 of Schedule 3 to the Disability Discrimination Act 1995" and

(c) in the definition of "relevant compromise contract" for "or section" substitute "section" and at the end insert "or section 9(2) of the Disability Discrimination Act 1995".

Companies Act 1985 (c. 6)

4. In paragraph 9 of Schedule 7 to the Companies Act 1985 (disclosure in directors' report of company policy in relation to disabled persons), in the definition of "disabled person" in sub-paragraph (4)(b), for "Disabled Persons (Employment) Act 1944" substitute "Disability Discrimination Act 1995".

Local Government and Housing Act 1989 (c. 42)

5. In section 7 of the Local Government and Housing Act 1989 (all staff of a local authority etc. to be appointed on merit), in subsection (2) –

(a) paragraph (a) shall be omitted;

(b) the word "and" at the end of paragraph (d) shall be omitted; and

(c) after paragraph (e) insert –

" and

(f) sections 5 and 6 of the Disability Discrimination Act 1995 (meaning of discrimination and duty to make adjustments)."

Enterprise aWSnd New Towns (Scotland) Act 1990 (c. 35)

6. In section 16 of the Enterprise and New Towns (Scotland) Act 1990 (duty of certain Scottish bodies to give preference to ex-service men and women in exercising powers to select disabled persons for training), in subsection (2), for "said Act of 1944" substitute "Disability Discrimination Act 1995".

SCHEDULE 7

Section 70(5)

Repeals

Chapter	Short title	Extent of repeal
7 & 8 Geo. 6 c. 10.	The Disabled Persons (Employment) Act 1944.	Section 1 Sections 6 to 14 Section 19 Section 21 Section 22(4)
6 & 7 Eliz. 2 c. 33.	The Disabled Persons (Employment) Act 1958.	Section 2

1970 c. 44.	The Chronically Sick and Disabled Persons Act 1970	Section 16
1978 c. 44	The Employment Protection (Consolidation) Act 1978	In Schedule 13, in paragraph 20(3), the word "or" in the definitions of "relevant complaint of dismissal" and "relevant conciliation powers".
1989 c. 42	The Local Government and Housing Act 1989	In section 7(2), paragraph (a) and the word "and" at the end of paragraph (d).
1993 c. 62	The Education Act 1993	In section 161(5), the words from "and in this subsection" to the end.

SCHEDULE 8

Section 70(6)

Modifications of this Act in its application to Northern Ireland

1. In its application to Northern Ireland this Act shall have effect subject to the following modifications.

2. (1) In section 3(1) for "Secretary of State" substitute "Department".

(2) In section 3 for subsections (4) to (12) substitute –

"(4) In preparing a draft of any guidance, the Department shall consult such persons as it considers appropriate.

(5) Where the Department proposes to issue any guidance, the Department shall publish a draft of it, consider any representations that are made to the Department about the draft and, if the Department thinks it appropriate, modify its proposals in the light of any of those representations.

(6) If the Department decides to proceed with any proposed guidance, the Department shall lay a draft of it before the Assembly.

(7) If, within the statutory period, the Assembly resolves not to approve the draft, the Department shall take no further steps in relation to the proposed guidance.

(8) If no such resolution is made within the statutory period, the Department shall issue the guidance in the form of its draft.

(9) The guidance shall come into force on such date as the Department may by order appoint.

(10) Subsection (7) does not prevent a new draft of the proposed guidance being laid before the Assembly.

(11) The Department may –

(a) from time to time revise the whole or any part of any guidance and re-issue it ;

(b) by order revoke any guidance.

(12) In this section –

"the Department" means the Department of Economic Development;
"guidance" means guidance issued by the Department under this section and includes guidance which has been revised and re-issued;
"statutory period" has the meaning assigned to it by section 41(2) of the Interpretation Act (Northern Ireland) 1954."

3. In section 4(6) for "Great Britain" substitute "Northern Ireland".

4. (1) In section 7(2) for "Secretary of State" substitute "Department of Economic Development".

(2) In section 7(4) to (10) for "Secretary of State" wherever it occurs substitute "Department of Economic Development", for "he" and "him" wherever they occur substitute "it" and for "his" wherever it occurs substitute "its".

(3) In section 7(9) for "Parliament" substitute "the Assembly".

5. (1) In section 8(3) omit "or (in Scotland) in reparation".

(2) In section 8(7) for "paragraph 6A of Schedule 9 to the Employment Protection (Consolidation) Act 1978" substitute "Article 61(3) of the Industrial Relations (Northern Ireland) Order 1976".

6. (1) In section 9(2)(a) for "a conciliation officer" substitute "the Agency".

(2) In section 9(4) in the definition of "qualified lawyer" for the words from "means" to the end substitute "means a barrister (whether in practice as such or employed to give legal advice) or a solicitor of the Supreme Court who holds a practising certificate.".

7. (1) In section 10(1)(b) omit "or recognised body".

(2) In section 10(2)(b) for "Secretary of State" substitute "Department of Economic Development".

(3) In section 10(3) in the definition of "charity" for "1993" substitute "(Northern Ireland) 1964", omit the definition of "recognised body" and in the definition of "supported employment" for "Act 1944" substitute "Act (Northern Ireland) 1945".

(4) In section 10(4) for "England and Wales"where it twice occurs substitute "Northern Ireland".

(5) Omit section 10(5).

8. In section 12(5) for "Great Britain" where it twice occurs substitute "Northern Ireland".

9. (1) In section 19(3)(g) for "section 2 of the Employment and Training Act 1973" substitute "sections 1 and 2 of the Employment and Training Act (Northern Ireland) 1950".

(2) In section 19(5) for paragraph (a) substitute –

"(a) education which is funded, or secured, by a relevant body or provided at
(i) an establishment which is funded by such a body or by the Department of Education for Northern Ireland; or
(ii) any other establishment which is a school within the meaning of the Education and Libraries (Northern Ireland) Order 1986;"

(3) For section 19(6) substitute –

"(6) In subsection (5) "relevant body" means –
(a) an education and library board;
(b) a voluntary organisation; or

(c) a body of a prescribed kind."

10. In section 20(7) for paragraphs (b) and (c) substitute
" or

(b) functions conferred by or under Part VIII of the Mental Health (Northern Ireland) Order 1986 are exercisable in relation to a disabled person's property or affairs."

11. In section 22(4) and (6) omit "or (in Scotland) the subject of".

12. (1) In section 25(1) omit "or (in Scotland) in reparation".

(2) In section 25(3) for "England and Wales" substitute "Northern Ireland".

(3) Omit section 25(4).

(4) In section 25(5) omit the words from "or" to the end.

13. In section 26(3) omit "or a sheriff court".

14. (1) In section 28 for "Secretary of State" wherever it occurs substitute "Department of Health and Social Services".

(2) In section 28(3) and (4) for "he" substitute "it".

(3) In section 28(5) for "Treasury" substitute "Department of Finance and Personnel in Northern Ireland".

15. Omit sections 29, 30 and 31.

16. (1) In section 32(1) for "Secretary of State" substitute "Department of the Environment".

(2) In section 32(5) for the definition of "taxi" substitute –
""taxi" means a vehicle which –

(a) is licensed under Article 61 of the Road Traffic (Northern Ireland) Order 1981 to stand or ply for hire; and (b) seats not more than 8 passengers in addition to the driver"

17. In section 33, for "Secretary of State", wherever it occurs, substitute "Department of the Environment".

18. For section 34 substitute –
"New licences conditional on compliance with accessibility taxi regulations

34. (1) The Department of the Environment shall not grant a public service vehicle licence under Article 61 of the Road Traffic (Northern Ireland) Order 1981 for a taxi unless the vehicle conforms with those provisions of the taxi accessibility regulations with which it will be required to conform if licensed.

(2) Subsection (1) does not apply if such a licence was in force with respect to the vehicle at any time during the period of 28 days immediately before the day on which the licence is granted.

(3) The Department of the Environment may by order provide for subsection (2) to cease to have effect on such date as may be specified in the order."

19. Omit section 35.

20. In section 36(7) for "licensing authority" substitute "Department of the Environment".

21. (1) In section 37(5) and (6) for "licensing authority" substitute "Department of the Environment".

(2) In section 37(9) for "Secretary of State" substitute "Department of the Environment".

22. (1) In section 38(1) for "a licensing authority" substitute "the Department of the Environment".

(2) In section 38(2) for "licensing authority concerned" substitute "Department of the Environment".

(3) In section 38(3) for the words from "the magistrates' court" to the end substitute "a court of summary jurisdiction acting for the petty sessions district in which the aggrieved person resides".

23. Omit section 39.

24. (1) In section 40 for "Secretary of State" wherever it occurs substitute "Department of the Environment".

(2) In section 40(5) for the definition of "public service vehicle" substitute –
""public service vehicle" means a vehicle which –
(a) seats more than 8 passengers in addition to the driver; and
(b) is a public service vehicle for the purposes of the Road Traffic (Northern Ireland) Order 1981;".

(3) In section 40(7) for the words from "the Disabled" to the end substitute "such representative organisations as it thinks fit".

25. (1) In section 41(2) for "Secretary of State" substitute "Department of the Environment".

(2) In section 41 for subsections (3) and (4) substitute –
"(3) Any person who uses a regulated public service vehicle in contravention of this section is guilty of anoffence and liable on summary conviction to a fine not exceeding level 4 on the standard scale.".

26. (1) In section 42 for "Secretary of State" wherever it occurs substitute "Department of the Environment".

(2) In section 42(1) for "he" substitute "it".

(3) In section 42(6) for "his" substitute "its".

27. In section 43 for "Secretary of State" wherever it occurs substitute "Department of the Environment".

28. (1) In section 44 for "Secretary of State" wherever it occurs substitute "Department of the Environment".

(2) In section 44(2) for "him" substitute "it".

(3) In section 44(6) for "he" substitute "it" and for "his" substitute "its".

29. (1) In section 45 for "Secretary of State" wherever it occurs substitute "Department of the Environment".

(2) In section 45(2) for "him" substitute "it" and at the end add "of Northern Ireland".

(3) In section 45(4) for "he" substitute "it".

30. (1) In section 46 for "Secretary of State" wherever it occurs substitute "Department of the Environment".

(2) In section 46(6) in the definition of "rail vehicle" for the words "on any railway, tramway or prescribed system" substitute "by rail".

(3) Omit section 46(7).

(4) In section 46(11) for the words from "the Disabled" to the end substitute "such representative organisations as it thinks fit".

31. (1) In section 47 for "Secretary of State" wherever it occurs substitute "Department of the Environment".

(2) In section 47(3) for the words "the Disabled Persons Transport Advisory Committee and such other persons as he" substitute "such persons as it" and for "he" substitute "it".

32. Omit section 48(3).

33. (1) In the heading to Part VI of this Act and in section 50(1) for "National Disability Council" substitute "Northern Ireland Disability Council".

(2) In section 50(2) for "the Secretary of State" in the first place where it occurs substitute "a Northern Ireland department" and in the other place where it occurs substitute "that department".

(3) In section 50(3) for "Secretary of State" substitute "Department of Health and Social Services".

(4) In section 50(7) for "the Secretary of State" substitute "a Northern Ireland department" and after "Crown" insert "or a Northern Ireland department".

(5) In section 50(9)(a) for sub-paragraphs (i) to (iv) substitute –

"(i) the Disabled Persons (Employment) Act (Northern Ireland) 1945;

(ii) the Contracts of Employment and Redundancy Payments Act (Northern Ireland) 1965;

(iii) the Employment and Training Act (Northern Ireland) 1950;

(iv) the Industrial Relations (Northern Ireland) Orders 1976; or".

(6) In section 50(10) for the words from "time when" to the end substitute "time when –

(a) there are no committees in existence under section 17 of the Disabled Persons (Employment) Act (Northern Ireland) 1945; and

(b) there is no person appointed to act generally under section 60(1) of this Act.".

34. (1) In section 51(1) for "the Secretary of State" substitute "any Northern Ireland department" and for "the Secretary of State's" substitute "that department's".

(2) In section 51(2) for "The Secretary of State" substitute "A Northern Ireland department".

(3) In section 51(4) for "a county court or a sheriff court" substitute "or a county court".

(4) In section 51(6) for "the Secretary of State" substitute "a Northern Ireland department".

35. For section 52 substitute –

"*Further provisions about codes issued under section 51*

52. (1) In this section –

"proposal" means a proposal made by the Council to a Northern Ireland department under section 51;

"responsible department" – (a) in relation to a proposal, means the Northern Ireland department to which the proposal is made, (b) in relation to a code, means the Northern Ireland department by which the code is issued; and "statutory period" has the meaning assigned to it by section 41(2) of the Interpretation Act (Northern Ireland) 1954.

(2) In preparing any proposal, the Council shall consult –
(a) such persons (if any) as the responsible department has specified in making its request to the Council; and
(b) such other persons (if any) as the Council considers appropriate.

(3) Before making any proposal the Council shall publish a draft, consider any representations made to it about the draft and, if it thinks it appropriate, modify its proposal in the light of any of those representations.

(4) Where the Council makes any proposal, the responsible department may –
(a) approve it;
(b) approve it subject to such modifications as that department thinks appropriate; or
(c) refuse to approve it.

(5) Where the responsible department approves any proposal (with or without modifications) that department shall prepare a draft of the proposed code and lay it before the Assembly.

(6) If, within the statutory period, the Assembly resolves not to approve the draft, the responsible department shall take no further steps in relation to the proposed code.

(7) If no such resolution is made within the statutory period, the responsible department shall issue the code in the form of its draft.

(8) The code shall come into force on such date as the responsible department may appoint by order.

(9) Subsection (6) does not prevent a new draft of the proposed code from being laid before the Assembly.

(10) If the responsible department refuses to approve a proposal, that department shall give the Council a written statement of the department's reasons for not approving it.

(11) The responsible department may by order revoke a code.".

36. (1) In section 53 for "Secretary of State" wherever it occurs substitute "Department of Economic Development".

(2) In section 53(1) for "he" substitute "it".

(3) In section 53(5) for "a county court or a sheriff court" substitute "or a county court".

37. For section 54 substitute –

"Further provisions about codes issued under section 53

54. (1) In preparing a draft of any code under section 53, the Department shall consult such organisations representing the interests of employers or of disabled persons in, or seeking, employment as the Department considers appropriate.

(2) Where the Department proposes to issue a code, the Department shall publish a draft of the code, consider any representations that are made to the Department about the draft and, if the Department thinks it appropriate, modify its proposals in the light of any of those representations.

(3) If the Department decides to proceed with the code, the Department shall lay a draft of it before the Assembly.

(4) If, within the statutory period, the Assembly resolves not to approve the draft, the Department shall take no further steps in relation to the proposed code.

(5) If no such resolution is made within the statutory period, the Department shall issue the code in the form of its draft.

(6) The code shall come into force on such date as the Department may appoint by order.

(7) Subsection (4) does not prevent a new draft of the proposed code from being laid before the Assembly.

(8) The Department may by order revoke a code.

(9) In this section –

"the Department" means the Department of Economic Development; and

"statutory period" has the meaning assigned to it by section 41(2) of the Interpretation Act (Northern Ireland) 1954.".

38. In section 56(2) and (4) for "Secretary of State" substitute "Department of Economic Development".

39. In section 59(1) after "Crown" where it twice occurs insert "or a Northern Ireland department".

40. (1) In section 60(1) to (3) for "Secretary of State" wherever it occurs substitute "Department of Economic Development" and for "he" and "him" wherever they occur substitute "it".

(2) In section 60(4) for "Treasury" substitute "Department of Finance and Personnel in Northern Ireland".

(3) For section 60(6) substitute –

"(6) The Department of Economic Development may by order repeal section 17 of, and Schedule 2 to, the Disabled Persons (Employment) Act (Northern Ireland) 1945 (district advisory committees).".

(4) In section 60(7) omit "paragraph (b) of", for "1944" substitute "1945" and omit "in each case".

(5) In section 60, omit subsection (8).

41. For section 61 substitute –

"*Amendments of Disabled Persons (Employment) Act (Northern Ireland) 1945*

61. (1) Section 15 of the Disabled Persons (Employment) Act (Northern Ireland) 1945 (which gives the Department of Economic Development power to make arrangements for the provision of supported employment) is amended as set out in subsections (2) to (5).

(2) In subsection (1) –

(a) for "persons registered as handicapped by disablement" substitute "disabled persons"

(b) for "their disablement" substitute "their disability" and

(c) for "are not subject to disablement" substitute "do not have a disability".

(3) In subsection (2) for the words from "any of one or more companies" to "so required and prohibited" substitute "any company, association or body".

(4) After subsection (2) insert –

"(2A) The only kind of company which the Department itself may form in exercising its powers under this section is a company which is –

(a) required by its constitution to apply its profits, if any, or other income in promoting its objects; and

(b) prohibited by its constitution from paying any dividend to its members.".

(5) After subsection (5) insert –

"(5A) For the purposes of this section –

(a) a person is a disabled person if he is a disabled person for the purposes of the Disability Discrimination Act 1995; and

(b) "disability" has the same meaning as in that Act.".

(6) The provisions of section 16 of the Act of 1945 (preference to be given under section 15 of that Act to ex-service men and women) shall become subsection (1) of that section and at the end insert – "and whose disability is due to that service.

(2) or the purposes of subsection (1) of this section, a disabled person's disability shall be treated as due to service of a particular kind only in such circumstances as may be prescribed."

(7) The following provisions of the Act of 1945 shall cease to have effect

(a) section 1 (definition of "disabled person");

(b) sections 2 to 4 (training for disabled persons);

(c) sections 6 to 8 (the register of disabled persons);

(d) sections 9 to 11 (obligations on employers with substantial staffs to employ quota of registered persons);

(e) section 12 (the designated employment scheme for persons registered as handicapped by disablement);

(f) section 13 (interpretation of provisions repealed by this Act);

(g) section 14 (records to be kept by employer);

(h) section 19 (proceedings in relation to offences);

(j) sections 21 and 22 (supplementary).

(8) Any statutory provision in which "disabled person" is defined by reference to the Act of 1945 shall be construed as if that expression had the same meaning as in this Act.".

42. (1) In section 62(2) for "Secretary of State" substitute "Department of Economic Development".

(2) In section 62(7) for "Great Britain" where it twice occurs substitute "Northern Ireland".

43. Omit section 63.

44. (1) In section 64(3) for "England and Wales" substitute "Northern Ireland".

(2) Omit section 64(4).

(3) In section 64(5)(a) omit the words from ", the British" to the end.

(4) In section 64(8) –

(a) omit the definitions of "British Transport Police", "Royal Parks Constabulary" and "United Kingdom Atomic Energy Authority Constabulary"
(b) in the definition of "the 1947 Act" at the end add "as it applies both in relation to the Crown in right of Her Majesty's Government in Northern Ireland and in relation to the Crown in right of Her Majesty's Government in the United Kingdom"
(c) in the definition of "fire brigade" for the words from "means" to the end substitute "has the same meaning as in the Fire Services (Northern Ireland) Order 1984"
(d) in the definition of "prison officer" for the words from "means" to the end substitute "means any individual who holds any post, otherwise than as a medical officer, to which he has been appointed under section 2(2) of the Prison Act (Northern Ireland) 1953 or who is a prison custody officer within the meaning of Chapter III of Part VIII of the Criminal Justice and Public Order Act 1994"
(e) in the definition of "service for purposes of a Minister of the Crown or government department" at the end add "or service as the head of a Northern Ireland department".

45. Omit section 65.

46. For section 67 substitute –

"*Regulations and orders etc.*

67. (1) Any power under this Act to make regulations or orders shall be exercisable by statutory rule for the purposes of the Statutory Rules (Northern Ireland) Order 1979.

(2) Any such power may be exercised to make different provision for different cases, including different provision for different areas or localities.

(3) Any such power, includes power –

(a) to make such incidental, supplementary, consequential or transitional provision as appears to the Northern Ireland department exercising the power to be expedient; and

(b) to provide for a person to exercise a discretion in dealing with any matter.

(4) No order shall be made under section 50(3) unless a draft of the order has been laid before and approved by a resolution of the Assembly.

(5) Any other order made under this Act, other than an order under section 3(9), 52(8), 54(6) or 70(3), and any regulations made under this Act shall be subject to negative resolution within the meaning of section 41(6) of the Interpretation Act (Northern Ireland) 1954 as if they were statutory instruments within the meaning of that Act.

(6) Section 41(3) of the Interpretation Act (Northern Ireland) 1954 shall apply in relation to any instrument or document which by virtue of this Act is required to be laid before the Assembly as if it were a statutory instrument or statutory document within the meaning of that Act.

(7) Subsection (1) does not require an order under section 43 which applies only to a specified vehicle, or to vehicles of a specified person, to be made by statutory rule.

(8) Nothing in section 40(6) or 46(5) affects the powers conferred by subsections (2) and (3)."

47. (1) For section 68(1) substitute –

"(1) In this Act –

"accessibility certificate" means a certificate issued under section 41(1)(a);

"act| includes a deliberate omission;

"the Agency" means the Labour Relations Agency;

"approval certificate" means a certificate issued under section 42(4);

"the Assembly" means the Northern Ireland Assembly;

"benefits", in Part II, has the meaning given in section 4(4);

"the Department of Economic Development" means the Department of Economic Development in Northern Ireland;

"the Department of the Environment" means the Department of the Environment for Northern Ireland;

"the Department of Health and Social Services" means the Department of Health and Social Services for Northern Ireland;

"employment" means, subject to any prescribed provision, employment under a contract of service or of apprenticeship or a contract personally to do work and related expressions are to be construed accordingly;

"employment at an establishment in Northern Ireland" is to be construed in accordance with subsections (2) to (5);

"enactment" means any statutory provision within the meaning of section 1(f) of the Interpretation Act (Northern Ireland) 1954;

"government department" means a Northern Ireland department or a department of the Government of the United Kingdom;

"Minister of the Crown" includes the Treasury;

"Northern Ireland department" includes (except in sections 51 and 52) the head of a Northern Ireland department;

"occupational pension scheme" has the same meaning as in the Pension Schemes (Northern Ireland) Act 1993;

"premises", includes land of any description;

"prescribed" means prescribed by regulations;

"profession" includes any vocation or occupation;

"provider of services" has the meaning given in section 19(2)(b);

"public service vehicle" and "regulated public service vehicle" have the meaning given in section 40;

"PSV accessibility regulations" means regulations made under section 40(1);

"rail vehicle" and "regulated rail vehicle" have the meaning given in section 46;

"rail vehicle accessibility regulations" means regulations made under section 46(1);

"regulations" means – (a) in Parts I and II of this Act, section 66, the definition of "employment" above and subsections (3) and (4) below, regulations made by the Department of Economic Development; (b) in Part V of this Act, regulations made by the Department of the Environment; (c) in any other provision of this Act, regulations made by the Department of Health and Social Services.

"section 6 duty" means any duty imposed by or under section 6;

"section 15 duty" means any duty imposed by or under section 15;

"section 21 duty" means any duty imposed by or under section 21;
"taxi" and "regulated taxi" have the meaning given in section 32;
"taxi accessibility regulations" means regulations made under section 32(1);
"trade" includes any business;
"trade organisation" has the meaning given in section 13;
"vehicle examiner" means an officer of the Department of the Environment authorised by that Department for the purposes of sections 41 and 42."

(2) In section 68(2) to (4) for "Great Britain" wherever it occurs substitute "Northern Ireland".

48. (1) In section 70(3) for "Secretary of State" substitute "Department of Health and Social Services".

(2) In section 70(8) for "the Secretary of State" substitute "a Northern Ireland department" and for "him" substitute "it".

49. (1) In Schedule 1 in paragraph 7(1) for "Act 1944" substitute "Act (Northern Ireland) 1945".

(2) In Schedule 1 in paragraph 7(7) for "1944" substitute "1945".

50. (1) In Schedule 3 in paragraph 1 –

(a) for "a conciliation officer" wherever it occurs substitute "the Agency"
(b) in sub-paragraphs (1) and (4) for "he" substitute "it"
(c) in sub-paragraph (3) for "the conciliation officer" substitute "the Agency".

(2) In Schedule 3 for paragraph 4(1) substitute –

"(1) In any proceedings under section 8 –

(a) a certificate signed by or on behalf of a Minister of the Crown or a Northern Ireland department and certifying that any conditions or requirements specified in the certificate were imposed by that Minister or that department (as the case may be) and were in operation at a time or throughout a time so specified; or
(b) a certificate signed by or on behalf of the Secretary of State and certifying that an act specified in the certificate was done for the purpose of safeguarding national security, shall be conclusive evidence of the matters certified."

(3) In Schedule 3 in paragraph 6(1) omit "or a sheriff court".

(4) In Schedule 3 for paragraph 8(1) substitute –

"(1) In any proceedings under section 25 –

(a) a certificate signed by or on behalf of a Minister of the Crown or a Northern Ireland department and certifying that any conditions or requirements specified in the certificate were imposed by that Minister or that department (as the case may be) and were in operation at a time or throughout a time so specified; or
(b) a certificate signed by or on behalf of the Secretary of State and certifying that an act specified in the certificate was done for the purpose of safeguarding national security, shall be conclusive evidence of the matters certified.".

51. (1) In Schedule 4 in paragraphs 2(1) and (5) and 7(1) and (5) omit "or sisted".

(2) In Schedule 4 in paragraph 4 for "Secretary of State" substitute "Department of Economic Development".

(3) In Schedule 4 in paragraph 6(1) omit "or, in Scotland, to the sheriff".

(4) In Schedule 4 omit paragraph 6(2).

(5) In Schedule 4 in paragraph 9 for "Secretary of State" substitute "Department of Health and Social Services".

52. (1) In Schedule 5 in the heading for "National" substitute "Northern Ireland".

(2) In Schedule 5 for "Secretary of State" wherever it occurs substitute "Department of Health and Social Services".

(3) In Schedule 5 in paragraphs 3(6), 5(1), 6 and 8(2) for "he" substitute "it" and in paragraph 3(7) for "his" substitute "its".

(4) In Schedule 5 in paragraphs 5(2) and 7(d) for "Treasury" substitute "Department of Finance and Personnel in Northern Ireland".

(5) In Schedule 5 in paragraph 8(2) for "each House of Parliament" substitute "the Assembly".

53. For Schedules 6 and 7 substitute –

Chapter	**Short title**	**Extent of repeal**
1945 c. 6 (N.I.)	The Disabled Persons (Employment) Act (Northern Ireland) 1945	Sections 1 to 4. Sections 6 to 14. In section 16 the words "vocational training and industrial rehabilitation courses and", the words "courses and" and the words from "and in selecting" to "engagement". Section 19. Section 21. Section 22.
1960 c. 4(N.I.)	The Disabled Persons (Employment) Act (Northern Ireland) 1960.	The whole Act.
1976 NI16	The Industrial Relations (Northern Ireland) Order 1976.	In Article 68(6) the word "or" in the definitions of "relevant complaint of dismissal" and "relevant conciliation powers".

INDEX